THE SUPREME COURT AND UNCONSTITUTIONAL LEGISLATION

BY

BLAINE FREE MOORE, Ph.D.,

Assistant Professor Political Science, George Washington University
Sometime Curtis Fellow in Columbia University

THE LAWBOOK EXCHANGE, LTD.
Clark, New Jersey

ISBN 9781584770992 (hardcover)
ISBN 9781616191474 (paperback)

Lawbook Exchange edition 2011

The quality of this reprint is equivalent to the quality of the original work.

THE LAWBOOK EXCHANGE, LTD.
33 Terminal Avenue
Clark, New Jersey 07066-1321

Please see our website for a selection of our other publications and fine facsimile reprints of classic works of legal history:
www.lawbookexchange.com

Library of Congress Cataloging-in-Publication Data

Moore, Blaine Free, 1879-1941.
The Supreme Court and unconstitutional legislation / by Blaine Free Moore.
p. cm.
Originally published: New York: Columbia University Press, 1913. (Studies in history, economics, and public law ; v. 54, no.2 = whole no. 133).
Includes bibliographical references.
ISBN 1-58477-099-6 (cloth : alk. paper)
1. Judicial review—United States—History. 2. Constitutional history—United States. I. Studies in history, economics and public law; no. 133.

KF4575 .M6 2000
347.73'12—dc21 00-044397

Printed in the United States of America on acid-free paper

STUDIES IN HISTORY, ECONOMICS AND PUBLIC LAW

EDITED BY THE FACULTY OF POLITICAL SCIENCE
OF COLUMBIA UNIVERSITY

Volume LIV] [Number 2

Whole Number 133

THE SUPREME COURT AND UNCONSTITUTIONAL LEGISLATION

BY

BLAINE FREE MOORE, Ph.D.,

Assistant Professor Political Science, George Washington University
Sometime Curtis Fellow in Columbia University

New York
COLUMBIA UNIVERSITY
LONGMANS, GREEN & CO., AGENTS
LONDON: P. S. KING & SON
1913

PREFACE

Although discussion of the unique position of the courts in this country has not been confined to recent times, probably never before has the question reached such an acute stage as at present, nor given rise to so much serious discussion as to the advisability of limiting some of the more important powers of the judiciary. An awakening consciousness of our social, economic and political defects and a growing belief that these can be lessened by increased governmental action has led to various reformatory measures on the part of the legislative and administrative branches. Whether wisely or unwisely we are not here discussing, but the fact remains that the courts, in some instances, have checked these legislative and administrative activities through their power to declare statutes and ordinances unconstitutional and hence null and void. This action on the part of the judiciary has caused wide-spread comment and led to proposals to limit, by various means, this power of the courts. In studying this question the author was struck with the fact that, although the courts are held responsible for many acts both wise and unwise, and individual cases are cited to prove the contentions set forth, yet no systematic attempt has been made to ascertain what as a whole the judiciary has accomplished by its power to declare statutes unconstitutional. It was to supply this omission that this study in one branch of the subject was undertaken.

In the text, though state cases have been discussed, an analysis has been made only of the federal statutes held void by the Supreme Court, but in the appendices an attempt has been made to list all cases in which state enactments were declared unconstitutional, by the same court, because of conflict with the federal constitution. It has been found very difficult to compile even an approximately correct list. Not only are the cases in question scattered among a large number of others, but additional difficulties were encountered. In some instances the information given in the official reports is scarcely sufficient to determine with exactness whether a statute has been annulled, or whether only an interpretation of it has been given. In other cases a statute has not been held void in words, but the judgment is in opposition to the statute and the result is to destroy the force of the act. In a considerable number of cases the act directly complained of and checked was that of an administrative body, but as in the majority of instances the state courts had previously held that such action was authorized by law, the conclusion is that a statute was in whole or in part held void. Also in various of the cases listed statutes were held to be void only as they applied to particular facts or a particular set of facts. In all instances, however, the activities of a state were checked, (which is really the important fact), because of conflict with the federal constitution, though in some few cases possibly a statute was not technically annulled. The list given may serve as a basis, and later investigations may correct any errors of omission or commission. The list has, however, been carefully checked, and, within the limits set forth above, an attempt has been made to have it as accurate as possible.

The author is indebted to Professor C. A. Beard who

has kindly read the manuscript and made many helpful suggestions; also to Miss Katherine S. Summy for aid in reading proof and revising it for publication. The author's thanks are especially due Professor F. J. Goodnow, both for his careful reading and corrections of the manuscript, and for many valuable suggestions and criticisms made throughout the preparation of the work.

WASHINGTON, D. C., *January, 1913.*

TABLE OF CONTENTS

PAGE

CHAPTER I

Early Attitude of the State Courts Towards Declaring Legislation Unconstitutional 11

CHAPTER II

Attitude of the Supreme Court of the United States Towards Holding Statutes Unconstitutional 35

CHAPTER III

Analysis of the Federal Statutes Held Void by the Supreme Court of the United States 77

APPENDICES

Appendix I. Table of Cases in which National Legislation has been Declared Contrary to the Constitution by the Supreme Court of the United States 129

Appendix II. Chronological Table of Cases in which State Legislation has been Declared Contrary to the National Constitution by the United States Supreme Court. 131

Appendix III. Statistical Summary of Unconstitutional Legislation 139

Appendix IV. Cases in which State Legislation has been Held Void by the United States Supreme Court Classified by States 142

Appendix V. State Legislation Held Void by the United States Supreme Court Classified according to the Constitutional Clauses with which the Legislation Conflicted 151

CHAPTER I

EARLY ATTITUDE OF THE STATE COURTS TOWARDS DECLARING LEGISLATION UNCONSTITUTIONAL.

THE doctrine that the courts can declare what is or is not law for the other co-ordinate departments of the government in cases coming before them in the exercise of their ordinary jurisdiction; that the courts can check the activities of the legislative branch of the government in instances where that will is determined by them to conflict with the fundamental written law,—all this has been so well settled in this country that until recently, perhaps even now—questioning that power or doubting the legitimacy of its origin has been regarded as almost sacrilegious. The firm position which this doctrine assumed in so short a time after it was definitely affirmed by the Supreme Court of the United States is a truly remarkable phenomenon.

The origin and growth of this immensely important idea in government has been traced by a few authors.[1] There may be some doubt as to just when and where the idea first appears, but it is quite certain that it was fairly well known at the time of the adoption of the Constitution, and consequently many years before Chief Justice Marshall rendered his famous decision in the Marbury case.

[1] Meigs, *The Relation of the Judiciary to the Constitution*, American Law Review, vol. xix, page 175. Coxe, *Judicial Power and Unconstitutional Legislation.* Austin, *American Historical Review*, vol. iv, page 456.

It is also quite correct to say that the doctrine that the courts may nullify an act of the legislature because in conflict with the constitution is distinctly American. It is true that in England a few rather sporadic attempts were made by the judiciary to assert the power of the courts to refuse to enforce a statute when it, in their opinion, was contrary to justice and natural reason. These attempts were made, however, not because of any power claimed on the part of the courts actually to nullify an act of Parliament, but because their duty as administrators of justice made it necessary to refuse to put into operation a statute which would, in particular instances, work individual hardships. As these statutes were not set aside because of a conflict with any definite superior law, but on the general grounds of incompatibility with natural right and justice and the fundamental rights claimed by Englishmen; and as obviously the idea of the constitutionality of statutes as it is known at the present time could not develop until after the advent of written constitutions, it is plain that these English cases can offer no exact precedents. Hence for the purpose of this discussion it will not be necessary to consider them, and we may pass at once to the development of the doctrine of declaring legislation void in American judicial history.

In the later history of the colonies the courts were told by counsel in some instances, especially the Writs of Assistance Case,[1] in 1772, that specific laws or the specific application of general laws might be contrary to common sense and natural justice, and that consequently

[1] John Adams' *Report of Otis' Speech*, C. F. Adams, *John Adams' Works*, vol. ii, p. 521. This and other material on the subject are collected in American History Leaflets, no. 32. Compare also the argument made in Robin *v.* Hardaway, Jeff. Reports 109.

the courts were under no obligation to enforce them in the particular case at issue. These arguments occurred in the colonial courts usually, though not always, when the controversies between the colonies and the mother country were up for judicial hearing, and the arguments of counsel in cases involving bitterly contested political issues are, of course, neither conclusive nor prima facie evidence that the courts had, or even claimed to have, such power. However, it was not long after independence had been declared and the various states had adopted constitutions that the courts began to assert judicially their power to declare a statute void should it seem to them to conflict with the constitution.

One of the very earliest, if not the earliest of the cases, which may illustrate this occurred in Virginia in 1778, when the legislature passed a bill of attainder against one Phillips.[1] About a year later Phillips was captured, indicted and tried by the regular procedure and no notice taken of the act of attainder. Whether this action was due to the discretion of the Attorney-General or to the refusal of the courts to recognize the attainder it seems impossible to determine.[2]

One of the very earliest cases in which it seems definitely established, although no opinion has been found, that the court declared a legislative act null because of conflict with the constitution is Holmes *v.* Walton, a New Jersey case decided in 1780.[3] New Jersey in an attempt to abolish the illegitimate trade with the British

[1] Hening's *Va. Statutes at Large*, vol. ix, p. 463.

[2] *Cf.* Burk's *History of Virginia*, vol. iv, p. 304, and Tucker's *Blackstone*, vol. i, part 1, appendix p. 293. See also Wirt, *Life of Patrick Henry*, appendix, p. 14.

[3] See Austin, *American Historical Review*, vol. iv, p. 456, for an extended account of this case. Referred to also in 4 Halsted, 444.

enemy passed a rather drastic act providing for trial in such alleged offenses before a Justice of the Peace in which a jury of six men might be had at the request of either party, and that in case a jury was used there should be no appeal allowed.[1] The case was originally tried before a Justice of the Peace, as the statute provided, and then came before the Supreme Court on a writ of certiorari.

The newly adopted constitution of New Jersey provided that "The inestimable right of trial by jury shall remain confirmed as a part of the law of this colony without appeal, forever,"[2] and the legislator's oath particularly provided for the protection of this section of the constitution.[3] As mentioned before, the opinion itself has not been found, but it seems established by circumstantial evidence that the statute was nullified on the specific ground that it was contrary to the constitution of the state,[4] and this too after mature consideration, the case having been carried over two terms of court. There is judicial evidence of this decision also for, in a case heard nearly twenty-five years later involving the power of the judiciary to declare a law unconstitutional, the Supreme Court of New Jersey said:[5]

At an early period of our government while the minds of men

[1] Act passed by the New Jersey Assembly, Feb. 11, 1775, Allinson's *Compiled Acts of the Province of New Jersey*, p. 468; also Wilson's *Laws of New Jersey*, Appendix v.

[2] Section 22, Thorpe's *Charters and Constitutions*, vol. v, p. 2598.

[3] Section 23, *ibid.*

[4] One proof of this is the fact that petitions were addressed to the Assembly protesting against the action of the court in having "set aside some of the laws as unconstitutional and made void the proceedings of the magistrates though strictly agreeable to the laws." See Austin, *op. cit.*

[5] State *v.* Parkhurst, 4 Halsted, 427, 444 (1804).

were yet unbiased by party prejudices this question was brought forward in the case of Holmes *v.* Walton. . . . There it had been enacted that the trial should be by a jury of six men and it was objected that this was not a constitutional jury; and so it was held; and the act upon solemn judgment was adjudged to be unconstitutional and in that case inoperative.

The court then continues that the act was repealed and the common-law jury substituted,[1] and concludes, "This, then, is not only a judicial decision, but a decision recognized and acquiesced in by the legislative body of the state."

It is true both that the Walton case was argued on the grounds that the statute was in conflict with the "Laws of the Land," and that the opinion is not extant, but the constitution was part of these laws and circumstantial evidence seems to warrant it being given as a case in which the constitutional question was clearly presented and as clearly decided.

In Virginia is found one of the earliest if not the earliest extant opinion[2] in which a court declared it had power to nullify a statute because of conflict with the constitution, and this power, though not actually used, was aggressively, boldly and rather gratuitously asserted. The question really at issue was whether in a certain class of cases a pardon voted by one House of the Assembly was sufficient. The clause of the constitution dealing with this subject was ambiguous, admitting of

[1] Shortly after this case was argued but before the decision was rendered the legislature passed an act (1779) allowing the justice of the peace to empanel a jury of twelve men if demanded by either party to the suit and after the decision was given in 1780, another act was passed requiring the justice on the demand of either litigant to grant a common-law jury. See Wilson's *Laws of New Jersey*, Appendices vii and viii.

[2] Commonwealth *v.* Caton, 4 Call, 5 (1782).

different constructions. The prisoner's counsel, however, injected a second question into the case, alleging that the legislature had, by another act, improperly limited the executive power of pardon, and hence the latter "statute was contrary to the plain declaration of the constitution; and therefore void." Although the case was largely or entirely one of interpretation, it was this last contention of counsel that gave the court its pretext for expressing its opinion on a delicate question which, it was unanimously agreed, was not necessarily involved in the point at issue. Wythe, J., speaking of the importance of conditions "when those who hold the purse and the sword, differing as to the powers which each may exercise, . . . the tribunals, who hold neither, are called upon to declare the law impartially between them," said:

Under these impressions I approach the question which has been submitted to us; and although, it was said the other day, by one of the judges, that, imitating that great and good man Lord Hale, he would sooner quit the Bench than determine it, I feel no alarm; but will meet the crisis as I ought; and, in the language of my oath of office, will decide it, according to the best of my skill and judgment.

I have heard of an English Chancellor who said, and it was nobly said, that it was his duty to protect the rights of a subject against the encroachment of the Crown; and that he would do it, at every hazard. But if it was his duty to protect a solitary individual against the rapacity of the sovereign, surely, it is equally mine to protect one branch of the legislature, and, consequently the whole community, against the usurpation of the other; and whenever the proper occasion occurs, I shall feel the duty; and fearlessly perform it.

The justice then states that when one branch of the legislature attempts to usurp powers,

I shall not hesitate, sitting in this place, to say . . . to the usurping branch of the legislature, you attempt worse than a vain thing; for, although, you cannot succeed, you set an example, which may convulse society to its center. Nay more, if the whole legislature, an event to be deprecated, should attempt to overleap the bounds prescribed to them by the people, I, in administering the public justice of the country, will meet the united powers at my seat in this tribunal; and pointing to the constitution, will say, to them, here is the limit of your authority; and hither shall you go, but no farther.

After this bold and by no means unduly modest assertion the learned justice closes his remarks,

This mode of considering the subject, obviates the objection made by the prisoner's counsel, relative to the constitutionality of the act concerning treason; for according to the interpretation just discussed there is nothing unconstitutional about it.

Pendleton, President, was not so sure as to the extent of the powers of the court as opposed to those of the legislature, though he recognized it as a "tremendous question," and confining his remarks to the case at hand, says: "I am happy in being of opinion there is no occasion to consider it upon this occasion."

The report of the case then concludes: "Chancellor Blair and the rest of the judges, were of opinion that the court had power to declare any resolution or act of the legislature, or of either branch of it, to be unconstitutional and void."

There can be no doubt that in this case an individual judge, if not the court, claimed for the judiciary as great, absolute and definite power as it has ever been able to reach or that has ever been claimed for it, and that this power was asserted when, according to the court's decision, there was no necessity whatever of expressing an opinion on the subject. Also there does not seem to have been any protest against this on the part of the public, possibly due to the fact that the theory, not being actually put into practice and hence void of concrete results, excited no general interest.

Probably the next case in point of time in which the judiciary refused to enforce a statute was Rutgers *v.* Waddington,[1] in the Mayor's court of New York in 1786. In a somewhat lengthy and learned opinion the court rendered a compromise decision, in which it refused to give an act of the state legislature full force and effect. The case was decided upon general principles of natural right, common sense and the laws of nations as laid down by Vattell, Puffendorf, and others, and the question of a direct conflict between the statute and a written fundamental law was not passed upon. Indeed the court says:

> The supremacy of the legislature need not be called into question; if they think fit *positively* to enact a law, there is no power which can control them. When the main object of such a law is clearly expressed, and the intention manifest, the judges are not at liberty, altho' it appears to them to be *unreasonable*, to reject it; for this were to set the *judicial* above the *legislative*, which would be subversive of all government.

But the court, following Blackstone, adds that,

> when a law is expressed in *general words*, and some collateral matter, which happens to arise from those general words is *unreasonable*, there the judges are in decency to conclude, that the consequences were not foreseen by the Legislature;

[1] Loudon's *The Case of Rutgers v. Waddington*, introduction by H. B. Dawson.

and therefore they are at liberty to expound the statute by *equity*, and only *quoad hoc* to disregard it.

Following this idea a compromise judgment was rendered which did not apply the statute to its full extent.

But this mild assertion by the court of its power to refuse to enforce the full letter of the statute was apparently not received kindly, for shortly afterwards at a meeting held in New York City a committee of nine was appointed to draw up an address. The committee accordingly prepared a memorial "To the People of the State of New York," scoring the court and asserting that "This proceeding, in the opinion of a good part of the citizens of this metropolis, and, in our opinion, is an assumption of power in that court, which is inconsistent with the nature and genius of our Government, and threatening to the liberties of the People." [1]

Shortly afterwards the question was brought before the lower House of the legislature and the clerk of the court ordered to produce the records of the case. The clerk complied, and after some debate the House adopted a resolution which first reciting the facts of the case and stating that the court had admitted a plea by the defendant specifically forbidden by the statute then,

Resolved, That the judgment aforesaid, is, in its tendency, subversive of all law and good order and leads directly to anarchy and confusion; because if a court instituted for the benefit and government of a Corporation may take upon them to dispense with an act in direct violation of a plain and known law of the state, all other courts, either superior or inferior, may do the like, and therewith will end all our dear bought rights and privileges, and legislatures become useless.[2]

[1] Dawson, *op. cit.*, p. xlv.

[2] Journal New York Assembly, 1782, p. 32, quoted in Dawson. See also McMaster's *History of the U. S.*, vol. i, p. 219.

Evidently neither the people nor the legislature was inclined to acquiesce in this asserted power of the court when an attempt was made actually to apply it in a concrete case as distinct from a mere statement of the theory.

The next case in which the courts asserted the doctrine of judicial nullification was probably the much advertised Trevett *v.* Weeden in Rhode Island in 1786.[1] This case is widely known partly because of the exciting contest being waged at the time between the paper and hard-money parties, partly because the legislature took cognizance of the matter and started proceedings looking toward the removal of the judges who rendered the decision, and also partly because the counsel for the defense made a long argument and then took the precaution to print his remarks so as to preserve them for the future. It is unfortunate from the standpoint of accuracy and fact that the arguments of the counsel rather than the opinion of the court are extant. The latter is not found and was probably only an oral one.

Rhode Island had passed an act compelling the acceptance of paper money, and providing for an immediate trial without a jury for anyone who violated the terms of the law. Wide publicity has been given this case and the position assumed by the court. Much of our information, however, is based entirely on the argument of the counsel for the defendant, and the defense made by the judges before the Assembly rather than on any exact record of what the court actually did or said. At all events there can be no doubt but that the court in a none too orderly proceeding refused to put the act into operation.[2]

[1] See pamphlet, *The Case of Trevett v. Weeden*, by J. M. Varnum who was counsel for the defense.

[2] See McMaster, *op. cit.*, vol. i, p. 337, for description of case and reference to contemporaneous accounts.

The aftermath was soon apparent, as in about a week a summons was issued from both Houses of the Assembly demanding the presence of the judges "to render their reasons for adjudging an act of the General Assembly unconstitutional, and so void."[1] Three of the five judges appeared and made their defense, and then influenced by some motive, possibly the fear of dismissal should the legislature pass on the merits of the case, the judges befogged the issue by diverting the attention of their prosecutors from the real issue to a new technical one, claiming it was not due process of law to dismiss them without specific charges and a hearing on those charges. With this showing coupled with the fact that the judges were elected from year to year by the Assembly and consequently had but a short time to serve, the case against the judges was dropped, but the Assembly "Resolved, that no satisfactory reasons have been rendered by them for their judgment on the foregoing information." It can scarcely be said, therefore, that the court won much of a victory in its contest with the legislature, or that the doctrine that the courts could declare a law unconstitutional gained much prestige because of its application in this instance. It is also worthy of note that in this case the court was not defending its own independence but was upholding private property rights.

Another Southern state was next to assert this right of the judiciary. A North Carolina statute provided that in ejectment proceedings the case should be dismissed on motion, if the defendant should make an affidavit to the effect that he had purchased the property in dispute from the Commissioner of Forfeited Estates. The judicial interpretation of this statute was first made

[1] *Records of the State of Rhode Island and Providence Plantations*, edited by J. R. Bartlett, vol. x, pp. 215, 218. Also quoted in Varnum.

in Den *v.* Singleton in 1787.[1] The court made every endeavor to persuade the parties to settle the controversy or submit to the usual trial by jury but without result.

> The court then, after every reasonable endeavor had been used in vain for avoiding a disagreeable difference between the Legislature and the judicial powers of the State, at length with much apparent reluctance, but with great deliberation and firmness, gave their opinions separately, but unanimously for overruling the aforementioned motion for the dismission of the said suits.
>
> In the course of which the judges observed, ... that notwithstanding the great reluctance which they might feel against involving themselves in a dispute with the Legislature of the State, yet no object of concern or respect could come in competition or authorize them to dispense with the duty they owed the public, in consequence of the trust they were invested with under the solemnity of their oaths.
>
> But that it was clear, that no act they, [the Legislature], could pass could by any means repeal or alter the constitution. . . . Consequently the constitution (which the judicial power was bound to take notice of as well as of any other law) standing in full force as the fundamental law of the land, notwithstanding the act on which the present motion was grounded, the same act must of course, in that instance, stand as abrogated and without any effect.

The case was then, notwithstanding the statute, tried by jury and verdict rendered for the defendant. In this instance the court not only asserted its theoretical power to disregard an act of the legislature which it deemed unconstitutional, but vindicated itself by actually exercising the power claimed.

The Virginia courts again asserted their power in a

[1] 1 Martin, 48.

case arising in 1788.[1] The legislature of that state provided that the Court of Appeals should organize the district courts. The act greatly increased the judicial and traveling burdens of the judges of the appellate court without any increase in salaries, and the judges asserted that in taking their stand they were simply protecting the independence of the judiciary from legislative aggression.

At the session when the district courts should have been organized the Court of Appeals did not follow the statute, but instead addressed a memorial "To the Honorable the Speakers and other Members of the Senate and House of Delegates of the Commonwealth of Virginia, in General Assembly." In this address the judges lamenting the fact that they must determine so delicate a question

> found themselves obliged to decide, however their delicacy might be wounded, or whatever temporary inconvenience might ensue; and in that decision, to declare, *that the constitution and act are in opposition and can not exist together; and that the former must control the operation of the latter.*

The legislature took no direct notice of the address, but did pass an act reorganizing the judiciary, and later the judges resigned their commissions as judges of the Court

[1] The Case of the Judges, 4 Call, 135. Possibly about the same time the Massachusetts courts claimed the same right but the only evidence of this seems to be a letter addressed to Jefferson by Thomas B. Cutting, under date of July 11, 1788. See letter in Bancroft's *History of the Constitution*, edition 1882, vol. ii, p. 472. Also *Proceedings of the Massachusetts Historical Society*, 2nd Series, vol. xvii, p. 507. Since there is practically nothing known about the case and it attracted no public attention or comment and has not been cited judicially as a precedent it is of but little value in tracing the development of the doctrine of unconstitutionality.

of Appeals, and some of them were appointed members of the reorganized court.

It is worthy of note in this case that the judiciary was fighting to maintain its own independence, and also that it was so uncertain of its position that it only called the attention of the legislature to the impossible position in which it was placed and asked for relief. Although the same court previously in Commonwealth *v.* Caton,[1] had made a bold assertion of its power, no mention is made of that fact in the present case.

A South Carolina court next took issue with the legislature, but in this instance[2] it can scarcely be said that the question of constitutionality in the modern sense was involved. A confusion of land titles had resulted, and in 1712 the legislature arbitrarily settled the matter, vesting the title in one of the claimants. When the case came up for judicial hearing the court said:

> The court, who after a full consideration of the subject, were clearly of opinion, that the plaintiffs could claim no title under the act in question, as it was against common right, as well as Magna Charta, to take away the freehold of one man, and vest it in another; and that too, to the prejudice of third persons, without any compensation, or even a trial by jury of the country, to determine the right in question. That the act was, therefore, *ipso facto*, void. That no length of time could give it validity, being originally founded upon erroneous principles.

It will thus be seen that the constitution of the state was not mentioned, the reasoning of the court following the English idea that the act was void because "contrary to common right and Magna Charta," and the

[1] 4 Call, 5, *supra*, p. 15.

[2] Bowman *v.* Middleton, 1 Bay, 252, 1792.

court did not avail itself of the precedents of sister states in nullifying a law because in conflict with the constitution.

In 1792 in Turner *v.* Turner.[1] and in 1793 in Page *v.* Pendleton,[2] the Virginia courts again considered the subject. The first case, however, was really one of interpretation, the court giving the statute a construction which it thought not inconsistent with the constitution, and contenting itself with informing the legislature that, "It is the business of the legislature to make the laws; and of the judges to expound them. Having made the law, the legislature has no authority afterwards to explain its operation upon things already done under it."

The second case dealt with the sequestration of debts due from Americans to British subjects during the war. It is a quaint opinion, and in reading it one is given the impression that the court had a preconceived idea of what justice required, and then called upon the laws of justice, of nature, and of nations to support that idea rather than resorting to the more direct expedient of nullification. Notwithstanding the language of the same court in Caton *v.* Commonwealth,[3] that case is not now cited nor does the court definitely draw the issue between the legislative and judicial branches, nor assert that the statute is contrary to, or set aside by any fundamental written law, yet its judgment is in direct conflict with the statute, and in effect the latter fails in its purpose. As yet even the Virginia judges did not quite have the courage of their indicated convictions, nor consider themselves securely fixed in a position which would

[1] 4 Call, 234.

[2] Wythe's Reports, 211.

[3] *Supra*, p. 15. For statutes construed in the case see Hening's *Virginia Statutes at Large*, vol. ix, p. 377; vol. xii, p. 529.

enable them definitely to declare a law void and worthless.

However, if the Virginia court wavered in its position in the preceding case, it again asserted its power in a contest following shortly afterwards, Kampfer *v.* Hawkins.[1] In a series of rather lengthy opinions the judges attempted to maintain the independence of the judiciary by coming out squarely against a statute. The legislature had given district judges power to act as chancery judges under certain conditions. The latter were provided for in the constitution and given life or good behavior tenure, while the district judgeships were statutory creations with judges having limited tenure.

Nelson, J., after discussing the proposition whether the legislature could alter the constitution and denying the charge that in nullifying a statute the court was assuming legislative power, concludes his opinion, "On the whole, I am for certifying to the court below, that the motion for an injunction be overruled, the clause under which it is prayed being unconstitutional."

Roane, J., after saying that at first he had believed that the courts had no choice but to follow a statute says:

> I now think that the judiciary may and ought not only to refuse to execute a law expressly repugnant to the Constitution; but also one which is by a plain and natural construction, in opposition to the fundamental principles thereof.

The learned judge then says that the court in attempting to maintain its constitutional position by declaring a statute void "will be censured by the ill-disposed part of their fellow citizens," yet the court must do its duty, and the integrity of the constitution has been upheld against

[1] 1 Virginia Cases, 20, 1793.

the legislature "by the repeated adjudications of this court." The opinion closes with the following: "From the above premises I conclude that the judiciary may and ought to adjudge a law unconstitutional and void, if it be plainly repugnant to the letter of the Constitution, or the fundamental principles thereof," and "I am of the opinion, that the clause in question, is repugnant to the fundamental principles of the constitution. . . ."

Tyler, J., says it is "truly painful" for him to pass on the question of constitutionality, but he cannot shirk his duty. He defends the power of the courts to declare an act of the legislature void if, in the opinion of the courts, it conflicts with the constitution, and to those who object to this doctrine he says: "A little time and trouble bestowed on this subject, I am sure, would enable any one endowed with common understanding, to see the fallacy of such sentiments." The judge then says he will not hesitate to compare the constitution and the statute and pronounce judgment as he may see fit, and concludes, "I concur therefore most heartily with my brothers, ... that the law is unconstitutional and ought not to be executed."

Tucker, J., says he will cite authority and precedent as part of his argument to sustain the position of the court. He refers first to legislative precedent, then quotes from the Federalist,[1] and finally takes up the Case of the Judges,[2] and cites that as a precedent for the present decision.[3]

[1] Federalist, no. 79.

[2] *Supra*, p. 23.

[3] The argument that the courts are the protectors of the constitution as against the legislature does not sound very convincing coming from this tribunal, as Judge Henry, who sat in this case, admits he is holding his position on the bench and performing his duties contrary to the constitution, but excuses himself on the plea of causing much difficulty should he refuse to continue.

This seems to be the first case on record where a court has attempted to maintain its position on this question by established precedent, though there were a considerable number of judicial opinions which might have been used for this purpose prior to this decision.

In the same year, 1793, the South Carolina court made some rather bold assertions in Ham *v.* M'Claws,[1] though rendering a decision really based on a liberal interpretation of the statute for this particular case, and the question of constitutional conflict was not raised.

In 1793 the Pennsylvania Supreme Court declared the judiciary had power to declare a statute unconstitutional, though without actually exercising the asserted right. The facts of the case[2] are somewhat complicated. One Austin was declared attainted and his estate forfeited to the state in 1780. The estate was sold to the plaintiff, who failed to make the required payments, and it thereupon presumably reverted to the commonwealth, and the legislature then attempted to pass title. The court, but one justice sitting, said: "But the act [presuming to vest title in the plaintiff] was repealed previous to the institution of this suit, . . . for the reasons particularly enumerated in the preamble thereof, and I have no difficulty in declaring for the same reasons, that the former act was *unconstitutional*." The court presents no argument to substantiate its power so to treat an act, nor

[1] 1 Bay 93. The facts in this case were as follows: South Carolina had prior to 1788 an act intended to limit slave importations but allowing actual settlers to bring in slaves for their own use. In 1788 slave importations were entirely forbidden and heavy penalties attached for violations of the act. The M'Claws with their slaves left British Honduras before the act of 1788 was passed but actually arrived after it was in force. The court refused to put the act in operation so far as this particular case was concerned and the jury found for the defendants.

[2] Austin *v.* Trustees, 1 Yeates, 260.

had this right ever been exercised by the Pennsylvania judiciary before.

Shortly after this the doctrine was apparently asserted and enforced in New Jersey in Taylor *v* Reading.[1] In a case[2] heard some years later the court in reviewing Taylor *v* Reading says that an act of legislature passed in 1795 "was by this court held to be an *ex post facto*[3] law, and as such unconstitutional, and in that case inoperative." But little is known of this case and apparently the only part it played in the development of the idea was to serve later as a precedent.

In 1799 the Pennsylvania courts again asserted what they claimed to be their constitutional power regarding legislation.[4] Acting under statutory authority, Philadelphia passed an ordinance prohibiting wooden buildings in certain sections of the city. The question of constitutionality was argued and after the court upheld the ordinance it could not forbear to say,

> As to the constitutionality of these laws, a breach of the constitution by the legislature, and the clashing of the law with the constitution, must be evident indeed, before we should think ourselves at liberty to declare a law void and a nullity on that account; yet if a violation of the constitution should in any case be made by an act of the legislature, and that violation should unequivocally appear to us, we shall think it our duty not to shrink from the task of saying such law is void. We however see no such violation in the present case, and therefore give judgment for the commonwealth.

In the foregoing the court gratuitously announced its

[1] Cited and a short synopsis given in 4 Halsted, 444.

[2] State *v*. Parkhurst, 4 Halsted, 427.

[3] The act was not a criminal one but a statute declaring that in certain cases Continental paper money should be received the same as specie.

[4] Republica *v*. Duquet, 2 Yeates, 493.

position since the statement on the question of holding legislation void was in no way essential to the decision —in fact was added apparently as an after-thought.

The Maryland courts were the next to claim the right to determine whether the legislature had exceeded its constitutional powers in the case of Whittington *v* Polk[1] in 1802. The question was whether the office of Justice of the Peace was included in the tenure of office guaranteed to the judiciary by the constitution. The court said that two constitutional questions were involved; first, is a legislative act contrary to the constitution void, and second, does the court have power to declare such an act void, and also stated that the two points were conceded by the counsel for the defendant. "Indeed they have not been controverted in any of the cases which have been brought before this court.

Notwithstanding these concessions, the court deem it necessary to communicate the reasons and the grounds for their opinion on those points." It is then held that there must be some power to decide such questions—the people can not because of practical reasons if for no other. "The constitution has placed the judiciary as the barrier or safeguard to resist the oppression and redress the injuries which might occur from such inadvertent or unintentional infringement of the constitution" and this power is properly vested in the judiciary, because it is independent and because the judges are appointed by the executive who, it is to be presumed, will appoint only upright and learned judges and, "without disparagement to the talents and legal acquirements of others," the judges will be those "who are better qualified and more competent than the rest of the com-

[1] 1 Harris & Johnson, 236.

munity." The opinion then closes with the statement that although the act is unjust, "The court are of the opinion that the said act is not void." Except the desire to claim the power it is difficult to see any excuse or justification for the discussion regarding the ability of the court to declare a statute void when that power was not involved in the decision.

In 1802 a North Carolina Circuit Court in Ogden *v.* Witherspoon[1] asserted the doctrine clearly that the courts would declare a statute void if in their opinion it came into conflict with the constitution either national or state.

In 1803 the doctrine of judicial nullification was elaborately presented by the United States Supreme Court and in such a manner as to settle definitely the question, so far at least as the federal judiciary is concerned, and to admit of practically no doubt in the future. We have seen that at least eight states, Virginia, New Jersey, New York, Rhode Island, North Carolina, South Carolina, Pennsylvania and Maryland, and possibly Massachusetts if we include a doubtful case, had asserted, prior to 1803, both the power and duty of the courts to compare the fundamental law and a statute and nullify the latter should they deem a conflict existed. The doctrine had been asserted more or less definitely in about fifteen[2] cases but in only eight of these, Holmes *v.* Walton,[3] Rutgers *v.* Waddington,[4] Trevett *v.* Weeden,[5] Kampfer *v.* Hawkins,[6] Den *v.* Singleton,[7] Page *v.* Pendle-

[1] 2 Haywood, 227.

[2] Seventeen cases are mentioned in the preceding discussion, but scarcely enough is known regarding two, the Phillips case of Virginia, *supra*, p. 13, and Taylor *v.* Reading in New Jersey, *supra*, p. 29, to justify any definite statements.

[3] See *supra*, p. 13. [4] See *supra*, p. 18. [5] See *supra*, p. 20.

[6] See *supra*, p. 26. [7] See *supra*, p. 22.

ton,[1] Bowman *v.* Middleton,[2] and Ogden *v.* Witherspoon was a statute really in whole or in part held void and the court actually exercised, in fact if not in name, the power it claimed.[3] We have already seen what happened to the judges in the Rhode Island case; the reception which the judgment in the Rutgers *v.* Waddington case had; that likewise the decision in Holmes *v.* Walton was received with protest though perhaps of a less violent nature than in any of the preceding. The court in Den *v.* Singleton rendered a decision which was roundly denounced, but the Virginia court seems to have escaped censure when it attempted to apply its theory. In one of these latter cases, Kampfer *v.* Hawkins the question was only that of the technical standing of the judiciary itself in which the public can not be expected to have much interest. History offers no great support to the contention that in early times the people quietly acquiesced in the judicial power to declare laws unconstitutional when that power was actually exercised in cases affecting the public.

One of the most remarkable facts connected with the position of the courts is that so many of them in a relatively short space of time claimed the power and claimed it aggressively and boldly, as the previous cases illustrate. In six out of fifteen instances in which the state courts had maintained they had power to declare statutes void, the opinions expressed on this delicate and important point were in no way essential to the decision rendered. In these cases there was an opportunity, not a necessity, for the courts to declare their powers, and

[1] See *supra*, p. 25. [2] See *supra*, p. 24.

[3] In the case of the judges, *supra*, p. 33, the statute was declared to be in conflict with the constitution, but this declaration was made in an address to the legislature and not in a formal opinion.

apparently at that time they never neglected such an opportunity.[1] More than this, at least so far as rendered opinions indicate, they were not following the precedents of sister states for, with the exception of Virginia in one case,[2] no court cited a precedent but worked out the idea as an original doctrine. Thus the principle that the courts can hold a statute void when in their opinion it conflicts with the written constitution grew up separately and nearly contemporaneously in more than half the states.

Also one is struck by the aggressiveness and confidence of the judiciary almost from the beginning of national independence. The courts proclaimed in no uncertain tones that they were the special protectors and guardians of the constitution; that it was their duty to guard against an executive and legislative despotism, seemingly assuming a judicial infallibility and seldom expressing any such fear, as was later expressed by a justice of the United States Supreme Court,[3] that such action might result in a "judicial despotism."

Moreover, the courts assumed, at least impliedly, that while both the legislative and executive branches of the

[1] The tendency to convert the ideas of the judges into bench-made law by inserting those ideas in opinions in which they are not necessary to the decision is still apparent. In the Standard Oil and Tobacco Trust cases, the Supreme Court of the United States in effect wrote the word "unreasonable" in the Anti-Trust Act. The necessity of the insertion of this in the decision is thus indicated by Justice Harlan: "Let me say, also, that as we all agree that the combination in question was illegal under *any* construction of the Anti-Trust Act, there was not the slightest necessity to enter upon an extended argument to show that the act of Congress was to be read as if it contained the word 'unreasonable' or 'undue'. All that is said in the courts' opinion in support of that view is, I say with respect, *obiter dicta*, pure and simple". Dissenting opinion, U. S. *v.* American Tobacco Co., 221 U. S. 193.

[2] Kampfer *v.* Hawkins, *supra*, p. 26.

[3] Justice Clifford dissenting in Loan Association *v.* Topeka, 20 Wall. 667.

government, particularly the former, are quite prone to overstep the bounds of their constitutional authority, they, the courts, will not do so, and that no check is needed to keep them within prescribed limits.

Also in these early cases, while the courts stoutly asserted and insisted that they were following the constitution, there is not a single claim in any case that the courts were exercising a power specifically given them by the constitution. Nor is there, with the single exception of the Kampfer *v.* Hawkins case, in which the Federalist is cited (and which refers to the United States and not the state constitution), any proof or attempted proof that such power was intended by the framers of the constitution involved. The courts were exceedingly zealous that the legislature should keep strictly within its constitutional limits, yet since the two branches are supposedly co-ordinate and of equal power, the means which the courts themselves used had no firmer constitutional footing than the very acts of the legislature which they were controlling.

It is difficult to find in history such an example of the assumption of power on the part of any branch of the government, and this is the more remarkable because found in a republic. It is certainly a compliment to the wisdom and efficiency of the judiciary of this country that it can claim such powers and exercise them to such an extent and yet escape with no more censure than the courts of this nation have received.

CHAPTER II

Attitude of the Supreme Court of the United States towards Declaring Statutes Unconstitutional as Indicated by Expressions in the Court's Opinions.

The previous chapter traces the development of the doctrine that the courts can declare a statute null and void if they deem it in conflict with the written constitution, up to the time this power was definitely asserted and exercised by the Supreme Court of the United States in Marbury *v.* Madison,[1] in February, 1803. But even the fact that the highest court of the land proclaimed and exercised this power did not altogether prevent censure and indignation when the same power was exercised by the state courts, for after 1803 there were protests, memorials and even impeachment proceedings when the latter courts thwarted the will of the state legislatures.[2] Although these local instances may be interesting and throw further light on the manner in which some of the claims of the judiciary were received by the public yet they are not within the scope of this discussion, which will hereafter be confined entirely to consideration of the doctrine of nullifying laws as it appears in the decisions of the Supreme Court of the United States or in the opinions of the Justices of that Court.

[1] 1 Cranch 137.

[2] See Baldwin, *American Judiciary*, p. 108 *et. seq.*

Before Chief Justice Marshall had definitely asserted this power for the United States Supreme Court, it had been suggested to, and argued before, the court and the Justices had expressed their opinions on the question in a more or less direct and official manner.

In discussing the topic of the power of the federal courts to nullify a statute because of constitutional conflict,—there always appears the moot question whether the framers of the constitution really did expect the courts to exercise the power which they afterwards claimed. One thing is of course obvious—the power is not specifically given in the constitution and if it is there at all it is one of those implied powers which the courts have worked out in the last century and a quarter with so much industry. Some of the more prominent of the members of the Constitutional Convention made statements to the effect that the courts were expected to exercise this power,[1] but the majority of them are silent on this point, and we have no proof other than certain circumstantial evidence that they acquiesced in such an important and novel doctrine. But however useful for certain purposes it might be if we were able to determine exactly what the framers and supporters of the constitution thought on this important point, such information would have little contemporaneous bearing on the early judicial opinions regarding unconstitutional legislation. The courts when they worked out the doctrine did not base their asserted power, so far as any thing in their opinions indicates, on the ground that it was any occult or hidden authority given or intended to be given by the framers of the constitution. It is true of course the judiciary claimed to find the power necessarily implied in the

[1] *Cf.* Beard, *The Supreme Court and the Constitution*, especially ch. ii; Dougherty, *Power of Federal Judiciary over Legislation*; Roe, *Our Judicial Oligarchy*.

constitution, but in few or none of the arguments do the courts attempt to justify their position by quoting the framers of the constitution, or citing constitutional documents originating immediately prior to the actual formation of the United states.[1] The courts were apparently willing to rest their case on the constitution itself and did not seek exterior proof to sustain them in their position.

The nullification of an act of the legislature is presumably a serious and delicate affair and the exercise of a power which the courts will use but sparingly. Has the Supreme Court of the United States always recognized this? Some light may perhaps be thrown on this subject and some idea of the attitude of the court towards the question may be gained by a study and comparison of the language used by this tribunal at different times, when approaching this momentous subject. Since the court obviously stands in quite a different relation to the legislatures of the states and the Congress of the United States, it will be necessary to divide the discussion into two sections, the first taking up the cases in which the validity of a federal statute was questioned and the second dealing with the same subject when a state statute was in doubt.

The federal judiciary had not long been organized when a constitutional question appeared before it. The first contest of this nature was Hayburn's case in 1790.[2] Congress had early provided that the federal judges should act as examining magistrates in regard to military pensions and their decisions were to be subjected to

[1] The only instance, so far as the author is aware, in which such documents were used in early constitutional cases is the quotation from the Federalist in Kampfer *v.* Hawkins, *supra*, p. 26.

[2] 2 Dallas, 409.

review by the Secretary of War.[1] The question was whether the judges had the constitutional power to act under these conditions. Although this case was never actually decided by the Supreme Court, as Congress kindly repealed the offending act so as to relieve, for the present, the embarrassment of the highest tribunal,[2] yet the question appeared before all but one[3] of the Supreme Court justices on circuit and they were thus compelled to express an opinion on what was then a doubtful question.[4] These expressions of opinion are presumably a very good index of the attitude of the judges at that particular time. The Circuit Court for the District of Pennsylvania consisting of Wilson and Blair, Justices, and the District Judge, made the following representation in a joint letter addressed to the President of the United States:

To you it officially belongs to 'take care that the laws' of the United States 'be faithfully executed.' Before you, therefore, we think it our duty to lay the sentiments which, on a late painful occasion, governed us with regard to an act passed by the legislature of the Union.

The court then points out the constitutional defects of the statute under consideration showing why it cannot act and concludes as follows:

These, Sir, are the reasons of our conduct. Be assured that, though it became necessary, it was far from being pleasant. To be obliged to act contrary, either to the obvious directions

[1] 1 U. S. Statutes, 243. [2] 1 U. S. Statutes, 324.

[3] The exception was Justice Johnson who although appointed November, 1791, did not qualify until August, 1792, by which time the Circuit Courts had expressed themselves upon the subject.

[4] *Cf.* article by Farrand, *American Historical Review*, vol. xiii, p. 281.

of Congress, or to a constitutional principle in our judgment equally obvious, excited feelings in us, which we hope never to experience again.

The Circuit Court of New York, consisting of Chief Justice Jay and Cushing, Justice, and the District Judge, after issuing a statement on the subject, so construed the act as to admit what it considered constitutional proceedings, but the Circuit Court for the District of North Carolina, in which Justice Iredell sat, found itself in greater difficulties and also addressed a letter to the President of the United States:

We, the Judges, now attending at the Circuit Court of the United States for the District of North Carolina, conceive it our duty to lay before you some important observations which have occurred to us in the consideration of an act of Congress lately passed, ...

We beg leave to premise, that it is as much our inclination, as it is our duty, to receive with all possible respect every act of the Legislature, and that we never can find ourselves in a more painful situation than to be obliged to object to the execution of any, more especially to the execution of one founded on the purest principle of humanity and justice, which the act in question undoubtedly is. But however lamentable a difference in opinion really may be, or with whatever difficulty we may have formed an opinion, we are under the indispensable necessity of acting according to the best dictates of our own judgment, after duly weighing every consideration that can occur to us; which we have done on the present occasion.

The extreme importance of the case, and our desire to be explicit beyond the danger of being misunderstood, will, we hope, justify us in stating our observations in a systematic manner.

The learned justices then explain that the constitution

provides for three separate and independent departments of government; that no department can enroach on the sphere of the other, and should this statute be acted upon a serious encroachment on the independence of the judiciary would result. After these explanations the address continues:

> These, Sir, are our reasons for being of the opinion, as we are at present, that this Circuit Court cannot be justified in the execution of that part of the act which requires it to examine and report an opinion on the unfortunate cases of officers and soldiers. . . .
>
> The high respect we entertain for the Legislature, our feelings as men for persons whose situation requires the earliest, as well as the most effectual relief, and our sincere desire to promote, whether officially or otherwise, the just and benevolent views of Congress, so conspicuous on the present as well as on many other occasions, have induced us to reflect, whether we could be justified in acting, under this act, personally in the character of commissioners during the session of a court; . . . .

The court, however, does not believe it can constitutionally act, but is exceedingly cautious, and later asserts that "if we can be convinced this opinion is a wrong one, we will not hesitate to act accordingly."

Evidently in 1792 the nullification of an act of Congress was not an easy moral task for the judiciary, and if the opinions of individual justices are an index of the attitude of the court, certainly the latter was in no way sure of its right or its power to nullify an act of the co-ordinate legislative branch.

The question of the constitutionality of a federal statute was first really presented to the Supreme Court of the United States in United States *v.* Todd[1] in 1792.

[1] 13 Howard, 52.

There is no complete record of this case either printed or in manuscript, the only official document being a certified copy of an extract of the judgment and a review of the case by the Supreme Court, printed as a note to a decision rendered almost sixty years after the origina case was decided.[1] Consequently this case throws no light on the attitude of the court regarding its power to nullify statutes, although it seems to have refused to exercise what it considered unconstitutional jurisdiction.

The next expression of opinion on this question by a justice of the Supreme Court, is that of Justice Paterson sitting on circuit in the Pennsylvania District in 1795. Justice Paterson in a charge to a jury in Vanhorn *v.* Dorrance,[2] in which a state statute was being reviewed, though the justice's remarks are general in their nature and not limited to the states, compares the relative position of the English courts and Parliament and then continues:

Besides, in England there is no written constitution, no fundamental law, nothing visible, nothing real, nothing certain, by which a statute can be tested. In America, the case is widely different; every state in the Union has its constitution reduced to written exactitude and precision.

. . . . The constitution is certain and fixed; it contains the permanent will of the people, and is the supreme law of the land; it is paramount to the power of the legislature, and can be revoked or altered only by the authority that made it. The life-giving principle and the death-doing stroke must proceed from the same hand. What are legislatures? Creatures of the constitution; they owe their existence to the constitution; they derive their powers from the constitution;

[1] United States *v.* Ferreira, 13 Howard, 39, 1851. Also referred to in Marbury *v.* Madison, 1 Cranch, 171.

[2] 2 Dallas, 304.

it is their commission; and therefore, all their acts must be conformable to it, or else they will be void. . . . . The constitution fixes limits to the exercise of legislative authority, and prescribes the orbit within which it must move. In short, gentlemen, the constitution is the sun of the political system, around which all legislative, executive and judicial bodies must revolve. Whatever may be the case in other countries, yet in this, there can be no doubt, that every act of the legislature, repugnant to the constitution is absolutely void.

This is a sweeping categorical statement that every act of the legislature exceeding constitutional power is bad and worthless. The learned justice does not, however, in any way attempt to prove or justify his assertion by any citations of previous cases nor by any specific clause of the constitution, nor does he attempt to show in any way that such power was intended by the framers of the constitution, but contents himself with claiming that such doctrine inheres in a written constitution.

In Hylton *v.* United States[1] a constitutional question was involved, but as no conflict was found between the statute and the constitution, the court did not make any strong statement in regard to its power of nullifying a statute and only very mild expressions of opinion on this point are found. Shortly after this decision came the great Marbury *v.* Madison[2] case in 1803 when a truly remarkable opinion was written. The timidity and uncertainty of the courts as to their right to exercise this power were by this decision forever banished so far as the federal judiciary was concerned. In this case Chief Justice Marshall has no apologies whatever for the position he is about to take, but assumes that the power of the court to nullify an act of the legislature, if in the

[1] 3 Dallas, 171.

[2] 1 Cranch, 137

opinion of the court that act exceeds constitutional authority, is an inevitable, inexorable consequence of a written constitution and of the theory of the American government. As the Chief Justice remarks:

> This theory is essentially attached to a written constitution, and is, consequently, to be considered by this court, as one of the fundamental principles of our society,

and he concludes his opinion with the following paragraph:

> Thus, the peculiar phraseology of the Constitution of the United States confirms and strengthens the principle, supposed to be essential to all written constitutions, that a law repugnant to the constitution is void; and that courts, as well as other departments, are bound by that instrument.[1]

There is no weakness manifested here, no hint of a feeling of delicacy or regret in thus deliberately thwarting the expressed will of Congress, nor is there any mention whatever of the supposed fact that the presumption is always in favor of the validity of the statute. If the Chief Justice had any qualms of conscience they are not visible in the opinion, which is confined largely to pointing out the limitations of the legislative body rather than indicating any particular respect for a co-ordinate branch of the government. Certainly credit must be given to the courage of the Chief Justice in trying this experi-

[1] Before he became Chief Justice, in arguing a case before the Supreme Court, Marshall declared that "The legislative authority of any country can only be restrained by its own municipal constitution; this is a principle that springs from the very nature of society; and the judicial authority can have no right to question the validity of a law, unless such a jurisdiction is expressly given it by the constitution." Ware *v.* Hylton, 3 Dall. 211.

ment; for considering the unfriendly attitude of the other departments of the government this was scarcely a propitious time for the court's aggressiveness, and so far as any assurances were concerned, the justices might have met the fate of the Rhode Island judges when they experimented with the same doctrine.[1]

In this case the Chief Justice avails himself of no precedents whatever, either state or national.[2] He does not by citation make use of any arguments previously presented on this point, nor does he attempt to justify his position by any of the records pertaining to the framing and adoption of the constitution, nor by any direct expression from any member of the Convention. Since the Chief Justice was, of course, thoroughly familiar with the history of the document, if the records pertaining thereto, as construed by contemporaries, afforded any substantial basis for the position now assumed by the court, it certainly seems fair to assume that the learned and astute Chief Justice would not have overlooked such excellent material for his opinion.

In some respects the action of the court in this case resembles that of the state judiciary in the earlier cases. In both instances the doctrine was worked out independently and separately without citing precedents even when those existed, and without attempting to show any specific or implied authority, except such as necessarily inhered in a written constitution.

Although in the preceding case the Chief Justice seems to have entertained no great conception of the

[1] *Supra*, p. 20.

[2] Both Hayburn's Case, 2 Dall. 409, *supra*, p. 37, and United States *v.* Todd, 13 How. 52, *supra*, p. 40, are referred to in the opinion, but the citations are used to support the argument in regard to the writ of mandamus and not to substantiate the constitutional contentions.

delicacy and solemnity of the court's action,[1] we find him in a later case expressing himself thus:

> To the general observations made on this subject, it will be observed, that as the court can never be unmindful of the solemn duty imposed on the judicial department, when a claim is supported by an act which conflicts with the constitution, so the court can never be unmindful of its duty to obey laws which are authorized by that instrument.[2]

After the case of Marbury *v.* Madison never again did Chief Justice Marshall have occasion to annul a Congressional act, and this power so boldly asserted in 1803 was not again used by the court until Scott *v.* Sandford[3] in 1856. In this case all the justices expressed opinions, and eight of them wrote long essays on the question before the court and on other matters, yet nowhere are there found any expressions of deference for the co-ordinate legislative body which passed the act, no statement that the presumption is in favor of the validity of a statute, nor any indication of regret that the court is thus drawn into conflict with Congress. The court had successfully defied Congress in 1803 and presumably it could again assert its claimed power.

In the succeeding cases, Gordon *v.* United States,[4] Ex

[1] As indicated by the following language: "The question whether an act, repugnant to the Constitution, can become the law of the land is a question deeply interesting to the United States; but, happily, not of an intricacy proportioned to its interest. It seems only necessary to recognize certain principles supposed to have been long and well established to decide it." Considering the temper and attitude of the Democratic administration at the time this decision was rendered, possibly the Chief Justice did not really take this matter so tranquilly as the above language might indicate.

[2] United States *v.* Fisher, 2 Cranch, 396.

[3] 19 Howard, 393.

[4] 2 Wall., 561; also 117 U. S., 697.

parte Garland,[1] and Reichard *v.* Felps,[2] the opinion of the court makes no mention of the delicacy of the question which it is considering nor any expression of regret or deference, nor is there anything in the opinions to indicate that the court presumed that the statute was valid.

In Hepburn *v.* Griswold,[3] the next case in chronological order, the court recognizes its peculiar position, for in approaching the question of constitutional validity it states:

> The delicacy and importance of this question has not been overstated in the argument. This court always approaches the consideration of questions of this nature reluctantly; and its constant rule of decision has been, and is, that acts of Congress must be regarded as constitutional, unless clearly shown to be otherwise.

After discussing the question and stating that, "Not every act of Congress, then, is to be regarded as the supreme law of the land; nor is it by every act of Congress that the judges are bound," the opinion continues:

> When, therefore, a case arises for judicial determination, and the decision depends on the alleged inconsistency of a legislative provision with the fundamental law, it is the plain duty of the court to compare the act with the Constitution, and if the former can not, upon a fair construction, be reconciled with the latter, to give effect to the Constitution rather than the statute. This seems so plain that it is impossible to make it plainer by argument. If it be otherwise the Constitution is not the supreme law.

The court then, by comparing the statute with the constitution determines that it is bad in part and having no

[1] 4 Wall., 333. [2] 6 Wall., 160. [3] 8 Wall., 603.

precedents to cite, original reasoning is depended upon to show the conflict.

In the three following cases, United States *v.* DeWitt,[1] The Justices *v.* Murray,[2] The Collector *v.* Day.[3] the court shows no hesitancy in nullifying a federal statute, makes no reference to the deference due to Congress nor does it in any manner indicate that the presumption is in favor of the validity of the statute. In the first of the three cases the court bases its reasons for nullification on an examination of the statute and constitution and simply states that the principle applied "has been so fully explained and supported on former occasions, that we think it unnecessary to enter again upon the discussion." In the Justices *v.* Murray the court depends almost entirely upon original reasoning to show the fatal defects of the law, having but a few remarks in the opinion of a single previous case to cite as precedent.[4] In the third, the statute is nullified and the decision is justified and upheld very largely by citing previous Supreme Court decisions. In United States *v.* Klein,[5] the court insists that the paragraph of the statute under discussion and which was nullified must have gotten in the statute by "inadvertence." The court shows no hesitancy in correcting this "inadvertence" of another branch of the government, but simply asserts that it is sure that it is fulfilling the deliberate will of the legislative body by refusing to enforce this part of the statute, but does not explain how it reaches this conclusion.[6]

[1] 9 Wall., 41. [2] 9 Wall., 274. [3] 11 Wall., 113.

[4] Parsons *v.* Bedford, 3 Peters, 447. [5] 13 Wall., 128.

[6] The portion of the statute annulled in this case was a rider attached to an appropriation bill of 1870. 16 U. S. Statutes, 235.

In United States *v.* Fox,[1] a Congressional act was nullified with little or no apparent reluctance and no mention of the fact that a statute is good unless a clear repugnance can be shown between it and the constitution. In the Trade Mark Cases,[2] the court recognizes definitely that it is dealing with a coördinate branch of the government, for it explains:

When this court is called on in the course of the administration of the law to consider whether an act of Congress, or of any other department of the government, is within the constitutional authority of that department, a due respect for a co-ordinate branch of the government requires that we shall decide that it has transcended its powers only when that is so plain that we can not avoid the duty.

In such cases it is manifestly the dictate of wisdom and judicial propriety to decide no more than is necessary in the case in hand. That such has been the uniform course of this court in regard to statutes passed by Congress will readily appear to any one who will consider the vast amount of argument presented to us assailing them as unconstitutional, and he will count, as he may do on his fingers, the instances in which this court has declared an act of Congress void for want of constitutional power.

After thus defining its position the court found the statute under consideration void.

In United States *v.* Harris[3] the court states:

Proper respect for a co-ordinate branch of the government requires the courts of the United States to give effect to the presumption that Congress will pass no act not within its constitutional power. This presumption should prevail unless the lack of constitutional authority to pass an act in question is clearly demonstrated. While conceding this, it must,

[1] 95 U. S. 670. [2] 100 U. S. 82. [3] 106 U. S., 629.

nevertheless, be stated that the government of the United States is one of delegated, limited and enumerated powers. . . . Therefore every valid act of Congress must find in the Constitution some warrant for its passage.

The court could not find any constitutional warrant for the statute discussed in this case and consequently it was null and void. After the above there follows a series of cases[1] in which federal statutes were annulled, all of them important and in two of them, The Civil Rights Cases[2] and Pollock *v.* Farmers' Loan and Trust Co.,[3] very grave questions were at issue; but with the exception of these latter two the court manifests no hesitancy in nullifying Congressional acts and has nothing to say regarding the deference due the national legislature but held the statutes void without any apparent judicial regret. In the two cases indicated above, which, if judged from the standpoint of public interest, are as important probably as any that have ever been before the court, some slight reference was made to the peculiar nature of the cases under discussion. In the Civil Rights Cases, in which the highest judicial tribunal was about to oppose its own judgment to that of Congress on an exceedingly important political question, the court refers to its relations to the legislative body in these words:

We . . . have felt, in all its force, the weight of authority which always invests a law that Congress deems itself competent to pass. But the responsibility of an independent judgment is now thrown upon this court; and we are bound to exercise it according to the best lights we have.

In Pollock *v.* Farmers' Loan and Trust Co., in which

[1] See Appendix I for list of cases.

[2] 109 U. S., 3.

[3] 157 U. S., 429, and 158 U. S., 601.

the court took an unexpected position and partially annulled the recently enacted federal income tax statute, it prefaced its discussion with:

Since the opinion in *Marbury v. Madison*, was delivered, it has not been doubted that it is within judicial competency, by express provisions of the Constitution or by necessary reference and implication, to determine whether a given law of the United States is or is not made in pursuance of the Constitution, and to hold it valid or void accordingly.[1]

Then after quoting from Chief Justice Marshall in the case cited, this portion of the discussion concludes as follows:

Necessarily the power to declare a law unconstitutional is always exercised with great reluctance; but the duty to do so in a proper case, can not be declined, and must be discharged in accordance with the deliberate judgment of the tribunal in which the validity of the enactment is directly drawn in question.

Instead of ignoring Congress or treating it with slight respect or consideration, the court in Fairbank *v.* United States,[2] in 1901 came back to earlier principles by opening its opinion with the following statement of its position:

The constitutionality of an act of Congress is a matter always requiring the most careful consideration. The presumptions are in favor of constitutionality, and before a court is justified in holding that the legislative power has been exercised beyond the limits granted, or in conflict with restrictions imposed by the fundamental law, the excess or conflict should be clear. And yet, when clear, if written constitutions are to be regarded as of value, the duty of the court is plain to up-

[1] 157 U. S., 554.

[2] 181 U. S. 283.

hold the Constitution, although in so doing the legislative enactment falls.

It is quite remarkable that the court feels it incumbent upon itself at this late date to support the above paragraph by citations, and yet more than a page is devoted to extracts from preceding cases, mostly from Marbury *v.* Madison, to justify a power which the court had been using, with no great hesitation, whenever it considered that occasion demanded, for almost a century.

In the decade following the decision of Fairbank *v.* United States, the court has in several cases[1] felt called upon to nullify Congressional acts. Yet, with but one exception, in none of these cases has the court expressed any hesitancy nor given any indication of the respect it is supposed to have for Congress, the one exception to the general rule being the Employers' Liability Cases, in which the court stated in an indifferently formal manner that, "Of course, if it can be lawfully done, our duty is to construe the statute so as to render it constitutional;" nor has there been in any of the cases mention of the fact that the presumption is always in favor of the validity of the statute. In most cases it has been left to the dissenting justices to bring out strongly the fact that an act of Congress is being nullified, that the court must have respect for the formally expressed will of the national legislature, and that the presumption is always most certainly in favor of the validity of the statute. But the court itself, after it has apparently determined to nullify a statute, usually fails to refer to this presumption, and the "painful difficulty" with which the early justices performed this task seems to have transformed itself into a habit which can be exercised by the court quite easily and without a twinge.

[1] See Appendix I for list of cases.

In the preceding section the discussion is confined, with but one exception, to those cases in which the validity of a federal statute was discussed before the Supreme Court of the United States, or to those cases in which the justices of that court expressed themselves on the right or duty of the judiciary to nullify such statutes if the latter appeared to conflict with the constitution. There are but comparatively few cases in which federal laws have been nullified and the great bulk of statutes which have been overturned by the Supreme Court are the enactments of the state legislatures rather than those of Congress. An attempt will therefore be made to ascertain the attitude which the court has had at various times towards nullifying state statutes, so far as this attitude may be ascertained from the language used in approaching the question.

One of the very earliest cases in which the legal force of a state statute was questioned before the Supreme Court of the United States was Ware *v.* Hylton.[1] In this case a Virginia statute, passed prior to 1789, conflicted with a subsequently ratified treaty of the United States which, under the constitution, had become part of the "supreme law of the land." The court was thus confronted with the delicate task of nullifying the state enactment. The opinions were delivered *seriatim* and the question was approached apparently with the greatest reluctance. Justice Chase expressed himself thus:

I have diligently attended to the arguments of the learned counsel, who debated the several questions that were made in the cause, with great legal ability, ingenuity and skill. I have given the subject, since the argument, my deliberate

[1] 3 Dallas, 199.

investigation, and shall, as briefly as the case will permit, deliver the result of it with great diffidence, and the highest respect for those who entertain a different opinion. I solicit, and hope I shall meet with a candid allowance for the many imperfections which may be discovered in observations hastily drawn up, in the intervals of attendance in court, and the consideration of other very important cases.

After making this plea for indulgence on the part of the reader or the public the Justice asserts, "I have already proved that a treaty can totally annihilate any part of the constitution of any of the individual states, that is contrary to a treaty," and "Our federal constitution establishes the power of treaty over the constitution and laws of any of the states."

Justice Iredell[1] states his opinion as follows:

In delivering my opinion in this important case, I feel myself deeply affected by the awful situation in which I stand. The uncommon magnitude of the subject, its novelty, the high expectation which it has excited, and the consequences with which a decision may be attended, have all impressed me with their fullest force. I have trembled lest by an ill informed or precipitate opinion of mine, either the honor, or the safety of the United States should suffer or be endangered on the one hand, or the just rights and proper security of any individual on the other. In endeavoring to form the opinion I shall now deliver, I am sure that the great object of my heart has been to discover the true principles upon which a decision ought to be given, unbiased by any other consideration than the most sacred regard to justice. Happy should I have thought myself, if I could as confidently have relied on a strength of abilities equal to the greatness of the occasion.

The court held that the Virginia statute was in conflict

[1] Justice Iredell had heard the case while on circuit, and now only re-read the opinion delivered in the circuit court.

with the United States treaty and consequently invalid. This decision, however, was only reached after a hard moral battle, by means of which the justices emerged from the "awful position" in which they had been placed.

In a case[1] decided four years later, 1798, the court was asked to pass on the constitutional validity of a state statute, in this instance one enacted by Connecticut in 1795. Justice Iredell in the course of his opinion stated:

> If any act of Congress, or of the legislature of a State, violates those constitutional provisions, it is unquestionably void; though, I admit, that as the authority to declare it void is of a delicate and awful nature, the court will never resort to that authority, but in a clear and urgent case. If, on the other hand, the legislature of the Union, or the legislature of any member of the Union, shall pass a law, within the general scope of their constitutional power, the court cannot pronounce it to be void, merely because it is, in their judgment, contrary to the principles of natural justice. The ideas of natural justice are regulated by no fixed standard; the ablest and the purest men have differed upon the subject; and all that the court could properly say, in such an event, would be, that the legislature, possessed of an equal right of opinion, had passed an act which, in the opinion of the judges, was inconsistent with the abstract principles of natural justice.[2]

In a later case,[3] in which it was alleged that a statute enacted by Georgia in 1782 was unconstitutional, Justice Chase expressed his opinion:

> Although it is alleged that all acts of the legislature, in direct opposition to the prohibitions of the constitution, would be void, yet it still remains a question, where the power resides to declare it void. It is, indeed, a general opinion, it is ex-

[1] Calder *v*. Bull, 3 Dallas, 386.

[2] *Cf*. Loan Association *v*. Topeka, 20 Wall., 655, 662.

[3] Cooper *v*. Telfair, 4 Dallas, 14.

pressly admitted by all this bar, and some of the judges have, individually, in the circuits, decided that the Supreme Court can declare an act of Congress to be unconstitutional and, therefore, invalid; but there is no adjudication of the Supreme Court itself on this point.

Justice Paterson thought, "That to authorize this court to pronounce any law void, it must be a clear and unequivocal breach of the constitution, not a doubtful and argumentative application."

In these cases the justices did not find themselves in any embarrassing situation, but contented themselves with saying that probably the court could nullify a state statute, but since it was not actually called upon to do so it was easy to escape from a position fraught with possible difficulties.

In United States *v.* Peters[1] the Supreme Court was brought into conflict with Pennsylvania and thought it necessary to declare void the action of the state. Chief Justice Marshall in closing the opinion in this case remarked:

> It will be readily conceived, that the order which this court is enjoined to make by the high obligations of duty and law, is not made without extreme regret at the necessity which has induced the application. But it is a solemn duty, and therefore, must be performed.

In this case the regret expressed was probably due partly to the fact that a statute was overturned and partly to the fact that the state of Pennsylvania had before this decision taken means to enforce the statute now nullified, but at all events the Chief Justice seems to have stood in some awe of the power of a "sovereign state"

[1] 5 Cranch, 115.

and have feared somewhat the shock of conflict with such a state. This, too, was about six years after the court had escaped uninjured when it exercised a somewhat similar control over the legislature of the nation which it was now exercising over that of a state.

The Supreme Court next checked the activities of a state legislature in Fletcher *v.* Peck.[1] Chief Justice Marshall, who delivered the opinion of the court, in approaching the question of constitutional repugnance stated,

> The question, whether a law be void for its repugnancy to the constitution is, at all times, a question of much delicacy, which ought seldom, if ever, to be decided in the affirmative, in a doubtful case. The court, when impelled by duty to render such a judgment, would be unworthy of its station, could it be unmindful of the solemn obligations which that station imposes. But it is not on slight implication and vague conjecture, that the legislature is to be pronounced to have transcended its powers, and its acts to be considered as void. The opposition between the Constitution and the law should be such that the judge feels a clear and strong conviction of their incompatibility with each other.[2]

It is somewhat remarkable to find the Chief Justice thus declaring so great a respect for the state legislatures and his great reluctance to vitiate any of their acts when the same Chief Justice had manifested no such reluctance or hesitancy when he nullified an act of the national legislature. Apparently Marshall had more respect for a

[1] 6 Cranch, 87.

[2] Justice Johnson in an opinion partly concurring and partly dissenting says: "I do not hesitate to declare, that a state does not possess the power of revoking its own grants. But I do it, on a general principle, on the reason and nature of things; a principle which will impose laws even on the Deity."

state than he had for a co-ordinate branch of the government of which the court, over which he presided, was an integral part.

The validity of a state statute because of a conflict with the national constitution was next questioned in New Jersey *v.* Wilson.[1] Chief Justice Marshall again gave judgment and in no way defined the position of the court on the question of annulling statutes, nor is there any indication of reluctance or regret. The learned justice simply stated that the statute,

in the opinion of this court, is repugnant to the constitution of the United States, inasmuch as it impairs the obligation of a contract, and is, on that account, void.

The Supreme Court next had occasion to nullify a state enactment in the case of Terret *v.* Taylor.[2] Justice Story in delivering the opinion of the court said,

that the legislature can repeal statutes creating private corporations, or confirming to them property already acquired under the faith of previous laws, and by such repeal, can vest the property of such corporations exclusively in the state, or dispose of the same to such purposes as they may please, without the consent or default of the corporators, we are not prepared to admit; and we think ourselves standing upon the principles of natural justice, upon the fundamental laws of every free government, upon the spirit and the letter of the constitution of the United States, and upon the decisions of the most respectable judicial tribunals, in resisting such a doctrine.

In this case the learned justice was not content apparently to rest his decision "upon the spirit and the letter of the constitution of the United States," but also needed

[1] 7 Cranch, 164.

[2] 9 Cranch, 43.

the additional legal and moral support of the "principles of natural justice and the fundamental laws of every free government."

The next case in which the court was called upon to decide an alleged conflict between a state statute and the United States constitution was in Sturgis *v.* Crowninshield.[1] Chief Justice Marshall spent no time in elaborating upon the delicacy of the situation, nor had he anything to say regarding the deference due a sovereign state, but simply asserted in a certificate to the lower court from which the case had come:

> This court is further of opinion, that the act of New York . . . is a law impairing the obligation of contracts within the meaning of the constitution of the United States. . . .

In the same term of court another constitutional question appeared in the very important case of McCulloch *v.* Maryland,[2] and Chief Justice Marshall again delivered the unanimous opinion of the court, but the Chief Justice was by no means insensible of the importance of the decision as indicated by the following language:

> In the case now to be determined, the defendant, a sovereign state, denies the obligation of a law enacted by the legislature of the Union, and the plaintiff, on his part, contests the validity of an act which has been passed by the legislature of that state. The constitution of our country, in its most interesting and vital parts, is to be considered; the conflicting powers of the government of the Union and of its members, as marked in that constitution are to be discussed; and an opinion given, which may essentially influence the great operations of the government. No tribunal can approach such a question without a deep sense of its importance, and of the

[1] 4 Wheat., 122. [2] 4 Wheat., 316.

awful responsibility involved in its decision. But it must be decided peacefully, or remain a source of hostile legislation, perhaps, of hostility of a still more serious nature; and if it is to be so decided, by this tribunal alone can the decision be made. On the Supreme Court of the United States has the Constitution of our country devolved this important duty.

After the Chief Justice thus fully states that he recognizes the seriousness of the action of the court and explains that the states have no power to burden the legitimate activities of the national government, he closes the opinion with:

This is, we think, the unavoidable consequence of that supremacy which the constitution has declared. We are unanimously of opinion, that the law passed by the legislature of Maryland . . . is unconstitutional and void.

The term of court of 1819 was an important one so far as constitutional questions were concerned, for scarcely had the court passed upon McCulloch *v.* Maryland when the equally famous case of Dartmouth College *v.* Woodward,[1] was decided. Chief Justice Marshall again delivered the opinion of the court, and that he was duly impressed by the importance of the court's action is attested by the following language:

This court can be insensible neither to the magnitude nor the delicacy of this question. The validity of a legislative act is to be examined; and the opinion of the highest law tribunal of a state is to be revised—an opinion which carries with it intrinsic evidence of the diligence, of the ability, and the integrity, with which it was formed. On more than one occasion, this court has expressed the cautious circumspection with which it approaches such questions; and has declared,

[1] 4 Wheat., 518.

that in no doubtful case, would it pronounce a legislative act contrary to the constitution. . . . In the same instrument [the constitution] they have also said, "that the judicial power shall extend to all cases in law and equity arising under the constitution." On the judges of this court, then, is imposed the high and solemn duty of protecting, from even legislative violation, those contracts which the constitution of our country has placed beyond legislative control; and, however irksome the task may be, this is a duty from which we dare not shrink.

And the decision closes:

It results from this opinion that the acts of the legislature of New Hampshire, ... are repugnant to the constitution of the United States."[1]

In Green *v.* Biddle[2] the Supreme Court had to act

[1] Justice Story, in a separate concurring opinion in this case, after stating that he believes the act under examination is unconstitutional and void continues: "In pronouncing this judgment, it has not for one moment escaped me, how delicate, difficult and ungracious is the task devolved upon us. The predicament in which this court stands in relation to the nation at large, is full of complexities and embarrassments. It is called to decide on causes between citizens of different states, between a state and its citizens, and between different states. It stands, therefore, in the midst of jealousies and rivalries of conflicting parties, with the most momentous interests confided to its care. Under such circumstances, it never can have a motive to do more than its duty; and I trust it will always be found to possess firmness to do that.

"Under these impressions, I have pondered on the case before us with the most anxious deliberation. I entertain great respect for the legislature [that of New Hampshire], whose acts are in question. I entertain no less respect for the enlightened tribunal whose decisions we are called upon to review. In the examination, I have endeavored to keep my steps *super antiquas vias* of the law, under the guidance of authority and principle. It is not for judges to listen to the voice of persuasive eloquence, or popular appeal. We have nothing to do, but to pronounce the law as we find it; and having done this, our justification must be left to the impartial judgment of our country."

[2] 8 Wheaton, 1.

again as an arbiter between the constitution of the United States and the enactment of a state legislature. Justice Washington, in delivering the opinion in the second hearing of the case, defined the court's attitude towards this question as follows:

Having thus endeavored to clear the question of these preliminary objections, we have only to add, by way of conclusion, that the duty, not less than the power of this court, as well as of every court in the Union, to declare a law unconstitutional, which impairs the obligation of constracts, whoever may be the parties to them, is too clearly enjoyed [enjoined] by the constitution itself, and too firmly established by the decisions of this and other courts, to be now shaken; and that these decisions entirely cover the present case.

After this assertion that the power of the court to annul a statute was now a fact established quite beyond question, the Justice indulges in a brief review of other cases along similar lines and closes his opinion:

As to the other branches of the government of that state, [Kentucky] we need only observe, that while the legislature has maintained the opinion, most honestly, we believe, that the acts of 1797 and 1812 were consistent with the compact, the objections of the governor to the validity of the latter act, and the reasons assigned by him in their support, taken in connection with the above case, incline us strongly to suspect, that a great diversity of opinion prevails in that state, upon the question we have been examining. However this may be, we hold ourselves answerable to God, our consciences, and our country, to decide this question according to the dictates of our best judgment, be the consequences of the decisions what they may. If we have ventured to entertain a wish as to the result of the investigation which we have laboriously given to the case, it was, that it might be favorable to the validity of the laws; our feelings being always on that side of the question, unless the objections to them are fairly and clearly made out.

The court, as indicated by the above, had no doubts at all about its power to nullify a statute, but was apparently very reluctant to use that power.

Following the decision of Green *v.* Biddle, several other cases in which the court had to pass on the constitutional validity of state statutes were presented to it, some of the cases involving important questions.[1] Although the court indulged in some explanatory remarks tending to justify itself and soothe the ruffled feelings of the states, it had apparently no great hesitation in nullifying the statutes; but in Ogden *v.* Saunders,[2] decided about four years after Green *v.* Biddle, certain members of the court in delivering their opinions *seriatim* again expressed their feelings of responsibility, as indicated by by Justice Washington's language:

I shall now conclude this opinion, by repeating the acknowlment which candor compelled me to make at its commencement, that the question which I have been examining is involved in difficulty and doubt. But if I could rest my opinion in favor of the constitutionality of the law on which the question arises, on no other ground than this doubt so felt and acknowledged, that alone, would, in my estimation, be a satisfactory vindication of it. It is but a decent respect due

[1] These cases were Society *v.* New Haven, 8 Wheaton, 464; Gibbons *v.* Ogden, 9 Wheaton, 1; Osborn *v.* Bank, 9 Wheaton, 738. (See Appendix II). Gibbons *v.* Ogden defined the relative powers of the United States and the states over interstate commerce and was consequently of great importance. In the inexorableness and certainty of its tone this case resembles Marbury *v.* Madison. Osborn *v.* The Bank excited considerable popular interest, but the general constitutional question affecting the validity of the state statute had already been decided in McCulloch *v.* Maryland, *supra*, p. 58.

[2] 12 Wheaton, 213.

to the wisdom, the integrity, and to the patriotism of the legislative body, by which any law is passed, to presume in favor of its validity, until its violation of the constitution is proved beyond all reasonable doubt. This has always been the language of this court, when that subject has called for its decision; and I know that it expresses the honest sentiments of each and every member of this bench.

Judging from this language as late as 1827, when this case was decided, at least certain members of the court still had great respect for a state legislature, and particularly avowed that no state act would be nullified except in case of the clearest necessity.

In Brown *v.* Maryland,[1] when the constitutionality of a state statute was again questioned before the Supreme Court, Chief Justice Marshall, in giving the opinion of the majority of the Justices, thus briefly alludes to the court's attitude on this point:

It has been truly said, that the presumption is in favor of every legislative act, and that the burden of proof lies on him who denies its constitutionality.

The opinion then closes:

We think there is error in the judgment of the Court of Appeals of the State of Maryland . . . because the act of the legislature of Maryland . . . is repugnant to the Constitution of the United States and consequently void.

These short remarks are all that the Chief Justice saw fit to insert in the opinion on this question.

In another case, Weston *v.* Charleston,[2] in which the court found it necessary to nullify a municipal ordinance because of conflict with the national constitution, Mar-

[1] 12 Wheat, 419.

[2] 2 Peters, 449.

shall again delivered the opinion of the court and while the Chief Justice seems reluctant to annul the ordinance, this regret was apparently not due so much to the fact that the court was thwarting the will of a local legislature as it was to the fact that the decision necessarily limited the taxing power of a state. Again about a year later in the case of Craig *v.* Missouri[1] where the court thought itself bound to limit the financial activity of the state of Missouri because of constitutional objections, the Chief Justice, delivering the opinion of the court, explains its position very definitely by the following:

In the argument, we have been reminded by one side, of the dignity of a sovereign state, of the humiliation of her submitting herself to this tribunal, of the dangers which may result from inflicting a wound on that dignity; by the other, of the still superior dignity of the people of the United States, who have spoken their will, in terms which we cannot misunderstand. To these admonitions, we can only answer, that if the exercise of that jurisdiction which has been imposed upon us by the constitution and laws of the United States, shall be calculated to bring on those dangers which have been indicated; or if it shall be indispensable to the preservation of the Union, and consequently, of the independence and liberty of these states; these are considerations which address themselves to those departments which may with perfect propriety be influenced by them. This department can only listen to the mandates of the law; and can tread only that path which is marked out by duty.

Thus the court, after it had asserted and exercised its power to nullify a state statute for more than twenty years, apparently did not yet find itself in such a secure position, or so free from censure as to be relieved of the

[1] 4 Peters, 410.

necessity of explaining and justifying its position before the public.

In another case, Worcester *v.* Georgia,[1] regarding a question deeply involved in politics and one which was bound to bring down much censure on the court should the decision be adverse to the state, Chief Justice Marshall was quite unterrified, simply explaining that the court could in no way escape making a decision in cases properly brought before it, as this was, and that it would decide according to its best judgment. But some of the other justices were not so sure of their position; for Justice McLean takes considerable pains to show that the constitution of the United States is the supreme law of the land, and consequently that no act of the legislature of any state or of Congress, which is repugnant to it, can be of any validity. Also the justice seems to think that the public has more confidence in the state than in the federal judiciary, for he shows that the state courts can and do nullify statutes of their respective states. Assuming that this power is beyond question in the state courts, the justice then by analogy shows that the federal supreme court must have the same power if a state act conflicts with the federal constitution. It is evident, however, that as late as 1832, the date of this case, the court exercised its power of nullifying state statutes with considerable hesitancy and trepidation.

Although the court undoubtedly had genuine hesitation in taking the action it did in Worcester *v.* Georgia, this case practically closes the period when it exhibits any great respect for a state legislature, at least so far as the language in the opinions indicates. In nearly every case up to the time that Worcester *v.* Georgia was de-

[1] 6 Peters, 515.

cided, the court, or at least some concurring member of it, has given expression to its recognition of the importance and solemnity of the proceedings, the deference due to a "sovereign state," and of the court's regret in being compelled to annul the act of such a state. But after about 1832 a change appears. In the fifteen years following, a considerable number of cases involving the constitutionality of state statutes appeared in the highest law tribunal of the land, and the court felt called upon, in various instances, to annul the statute in question.[1] Some of the questions involved were not particularly important, and most of the opinions during these years are short. But there were also some really important questions argued before the court—questions which had wide-reaching influence on the activities of the states—and yet the court declared these statutes unconstitutional without any apparent hesitancy and with few expressions of regret because they were forced to take such action. During this period the dignity of the state, the deference due to that government, the presumption of constitutionality and the warning that "there is no portion of the power and jurisdiction committed to this court which demands so much caution in its exercise, as that of declaring the legislation of a state to be null and void, because it comes in conflict with the Constitution of the United States,"[2] all found refuge in that haven of possibilities but not actualities—dissenting opinions.

During the years immediately preceding and following the Civil War the court in approaching a question of a constitutional nature assumed an attitude of indifference. Its opinions in constitutional cases are short

[1] See Appendix II for list of these cases.

[2] Dissenting opinion, Woodruff *v.* Trapnell, 10 Howard, 209.

usually, and but little or no space is wasted in softening its decisions, the court simply making some blunt statement that the statute is invalid.

In the case of Inman Steamship Co. *v.* Tinker,[1] the court in a short five-page decision makes the brief statement:

> The State, in passing this law imposing a tonnage duty, has exercised a power expressly prohibited to it by the Constitution. In that particular the law is, therefore, void.

Again in Foster *v.* New Orleans,[2] in an opinion covering less than three pages, in describing certain duties levied by the legislature of Louisiana, at the port of New Orleans, the court states:

> They [the provisions of the statute] are a clog and a blow to all such commerce in the port to which they relate. Their enactment involved a power which belongs exclusively to Congress, and which a state could not, therefore, properly exercise. . . . We hold the statute to be void.

In Guy *v.* Baltimore,[3] in which both the statute of the state of Maryland and an ordinance of the city of Baltimore were questioned, the court used no space in stating its respect for the legislative will of a state or city, but disposes of the matter with this short and definite statement:

> Nothing can be clearer than that the statute of the state of Maryland and the ordinance of the city of Baltimore, in the respects adverted to, are in conflict with the power of Congress over the subject of commerce.

For constitutional cases the record for brevity and con-

[1] 94 U. S., 238. [2] 94 U. S., 246. [3] 100 U. S., 434.

ciseness, so far as the Supreme Court is concerned, is probably held by the case of the Adams Express Company *v.* Kentucky.[1] In a decision covering two pages a statute of the state is partially annulled, the court indicating its attitude towards the constitutional question by the following language:[2] "Clearly within the cases above cited the statute before us as applied to transportation from State to State cannot be sustained."

In the cases previously mentioned, while the court's opinions were quite short and curt and but scant respect was shown to the states, and the court did not see fit to express any regrets that they were compelled by their sense of duty to annul statutes, yet there is no doubt that in each case a statute is annulled, the court distinctly stating so. Also the court indicated the clause of the constitution with which the statute conflicted, or if there was no specific clause it took pains to show why the statute was contrary to the spirit of the constitution. There is, however, another class of cases in which, while the judgment was distinctly contrary to the statute in question, the court did not apparently think it of sufficient importance to mention the fact that a state statute was being annulled. In Hawthorne *v.* Calef[3] the court makes no mention of the fact that a statute is being declared void. Seemingly the court is entirely occupied with its reasoning, and the nullification of a state statute is an incidental or a by-product which is not mentioned.

In Hall *v.* Wisconsin[4] the court again nullifies the will

[1] 214 U. S., 218.

[2] Several of these short, concise opinions in constitutional cases have appeared very recently. See Dozier *v.* Alabama, 218 U. S., 124; Railroad Co. *v.* O'Connor, 223 U. S., 280; Oklahoma *v.* Wells, Fargo & Co., 223 U. S., 298.

[3] 2 Wall., 10.

[4] 103 U. S., 5.

of a state legislature, though not doing so in express terms. There is a considerable number of cases[1] where the court did not take the trouble to mention the fact that a statute was being vitiated, or did so only incidentally, leaving its judgments to work out the inevitable nullifying effect.[2]

It certainly is indicative of the great growth of judicial power in this country that the same tribunal which found itself involved in so much difficulty, pain and travail in the earlier period of its existence could later so nonchalantly nullify state enactments.

In the above cases while the court neglected to pay any particular respect to the states and apparently had no great reluctance in nullifying state statutes yet it said nothing derogatory of the state legislatures. There are cases, however, in which the court has not been so kindly in its attitude towards the states and their law-making bodies. In some instances it has scolded them and manifested impatience towards them; in others it has assumed a somewhat patronizing air and finally in others indulged in hostile criticism, in some cases quite bitter.

One of the first cases in which this attitude appears is Curran *v* Arkansas.[3] It was alleged that the state of Arkansas had made a contract and then later attempted

[1] E. g. Dunphy *v.* Kleinsmith, 11 Wall., 610 (territorial statute); Delmas *v.* Merchants Insurance Co., 14 Wall., 661; Cook *v.* Pennsylvania, 97 U. S., 566; University *v.* The People, 99 U. S., 309; Nelson *v.* Parish of St. Martin, 111 U. S., 716.

[2] In Neilson *v.* Oregon, 212 U. S., 315, the court does not attempt any constitutional discussion of any sort, but does partly annul an act of Oregon, simply saying that the state can not do what it has attempted, and presumably expects justification for its decision from the peculiar circumstances surrounding the case.

[3] 15 Howard, 304 (1853).

to impair the obligation of that contract. Speaking of this the court says:

The obligation of such a contract can no more be impaired than if it were under no circumstances subject to legislative control. The assumption that, because the legislature may destroy a contract by repealing the charter of the corporation which made it, therefore such a contract may be impaired, or altered, or destroyed, in any manner the legislature may think fit, without repealing the charter, is wholly inadmissable.

In Wilmington *v.* Reid[1] the court manifests its impatience regarding the state of North Carolina because it has again to express itself on a principle which it has had great difficulty in forcing the states to accept, namely, that a public corporation can make an agreement which the same organ of the corporation may not later repeal, or in other words that a state or municipal corporation may make an irrepealable contract and be bound by the rules of private law. In this case the court opens its argument with:

It has been so often decided by this court that a charter of incorporation granted by a State creates a contract between the State and the corporators, which the State cannot violate, that it would be a work of supererogation to repeat the reasons on which the argument is founded. . . . If, however, the contract is plain and unambiguous, and the meaning of the parties to it can be clearly ascertained, it is the duty of the court to give effect to it, the same as if it were a contract between private persons, without regard to its supposed injurious effects upon the public interest.[2]

[1] 13 Wall., 264.

[2] In this case the court continued the argument as follows: "It may be conceded that it were better for the interest of the State, that the

In Gunn *v*. Barry,[1] a Georgia statute is annulled and the court accuses the legislature of committing a serious offense in passing such a statute for it says in part:

The effect of the act in question, under the circumstances of this judgment, does not indeed merely impair, it annihilates the remedy. There is none left.

But the act reaches still further. . . . It is in effect taking one person's property and giving it to another without compensation. This is contrary to reason and justice and to the fundamental principles of the social compact. But we must confine ourselves to the constitutional aspect of the case.

Certainly the court shows no great respect for a state legislature when it accuses that body of deliberately purloining property.

In the case of State Tax on Foreign Held Bonds,[2] the court makes a similar attack on the legislature of another state and in this latter instance an attack not on one of the discredited Southern states either, but on Pennsylvania.

taxing power, which is one of the highest and most important attributes of sovereignty, should on no occasion be surrendered. . . . But the courts of the country are not the proper tribunals to apply the corrective to improvident legislation of this character. If there be no constitutional restraint on the action of the Legislature on this subject, there is no remedy, except through the influence of a wise public sentiment, reaching and controlling the conduct of the law-making power." The Supreme Court seems quite to forget it was that body itself, and not the legislatures, that made these so-called contracts irrepealable and inviolable, and that "a wise public sentiment" can in no way affect a grant or contract once made irrepealable or perpetual by the judiciary. Here the court throws the whole burden of responsibility on the legislature and says nothing about its share in bringing about the undesirable conditions presented by this case.

[1] 15 Wall., 610.

[2] 15 Wall., 300.

In Louisiana *v.* Pilsbury[1] the court pays its respects to the legislature of Louisiana in these words:

We shall not waste words upon the scheme thus developed to evade the just obligation of the city. Notwithstanding the declaration in the preamble, that the act seeks from the creditors the indulgence necessary "for the public well-being and the maintenance of the public honor," it is, so far as the consolidated bonds are concerned, tainted with the leprosy of repudiation. . . . The primal duty of the city authorities to fulfill punctually their obligations and maintain good faith is thus proclaimed to be no duty at all.

In the Virginia Coupon Cases[2] the court becomes quite patronizing,[3] and in Loan Association *v.* Topeka,[4] though the court could find no specific clause of the constitution which was violated, still it was quite sure that the Kansas statute was void, and expresses its opinion of the action of the legislature of that state as follows:

To lay with one hand the power of the government on the property of a citizen, and with the other to bestow it upon favored individuals to aid private enterprises and build up

[1] 105 U. S., 278. [2] 114 U. S., 269.

[3] In Collins *v.* New Hampshire, 171 U. S., 30, the court becomes facetious. New Hampshire had provided that all oleomargarine in order to be sold legally in the state must be colored pink. The court in expressing its opinion on this part of the statute says: "If this provision for coloring the article were a legal condition, a legislature could not be limited to pink in its choice of colors. The legislative fancy or taste would be boundless. It might equally as well provide that it should be colored blue or red or black." Is it possible to imagine the court of Marshall, Washington, Mclean or Iredell, when confronted with a question involving the constitutionality of a state statute, discussing the state legislators' artistic sense as to whether an article of commerce should be dyed blue or red or black?

[4] 20 Wall., 655.

private fortunes, is none the less robbery because it is done under the forms of law and is called taxation. This is not legislation. It is a decree under legislative forms.[1]

The court in this instance, in plain language, accuses the legislature of a felonious act, and it is difficult to harmonize such sentiments with the great respect which the

[1] In Houston and Central Railroad Co. *v*. Texas, 177 U. S., 66, the court by a tortuous course of reasoning claimed jurisdiction and gave a curious twist to its old doctrine of respect for the legislature. The facts of the case are somewhat complicated, but briefly the railroads of Texas found themselves in financial distress during the Civil War and the state in rendering aid allowed them to pay off certain claims due the state by evidence of indebtedness issued by the state during the war and called treasury warrants. Afterwards the state refused to allow the railroads credit for the amount of the warrants thus paid on the ground that the law authorizing the issue of the latter was unconstitutional and void. When the case came on for trial the court again became solicitous about the dignity of a state legislature, not, however, that it might show respect for the state, but because by upholding the original act of the Texas legislature it might thus protect the property rights of the railroad. In the course of its opinion in this case the court states:

"A deliberate intention on the part of a legislative body to violate the organic law of the state under which it exists and to which the members have sworn obedience, is not to be lightly indulged. The existence of such intention should be proved beyond doubt or cavil from the very acts themselves which are under discussion, and if it be reasonably possible to construe them so as to render them valid, a proper respect for the legislative department calls for such construction rather than one which invalidates them, because they were enacted with a direct purpose to violate the state constitution."

This language sounds familiar, but the purpose for which it is used is widely different from that for which similar words were employed half or three-quarters of a century earlier. Also it is to be noted that while the court, with a great show of respect for the state legislature, refused to nullify the original act, thus protecting the railroad, it manifested no such compunction when it annulled the later statute which as construed by the state authorities took away from the railroads the benefits of the original law. The respect which the judiciary is supposed to have for the legislature can be made to serve a variety of purposes.

court in some of its earlier opinions professed to have for the state law-making bodies.

In Smyth *v*. Ames,[1] the court seems to have quite reversed its ancient attitude in approaching this question, as witness:

No one, we take it, will contend that a state enactment is in harmony with that law [the constitution] simply because the legislature of the State has declared such to be the case; for that would make the state legislature the final judge of the validity of its enactment, although the Constitution of the United States and the laws made in pursuance thereof are the supreme law of the land, anything in the constitution and laws of the state nothwithstanding.[2]

[1] 169 U. S., 466, 527.

[2] This opinion continues: "The idea that any legislature, state or Federal, can conclusively determine for the people and for the courts that what it enacts in the form of law, or what it authorizes its agents to do, is consistent with the fundamental law, is in opposition to the theory of our institutions. The duty rests upon all courts, Federal and state, when their jurisdiction is properly invoked, to see to it that no right secured by the supreme law of the land is impaired or destroyed by legislation. This function and duty of the judiciary distinguishes the American system from all other systems of government. The perpetuity of our institutions and the liberty which is enjoyed under them depend, in no small degree, upon the power given to the judiciary to declare null and void all legislation that is clearly repugnant to the supreme law of the land."

This is the judiciary's attitude regarding its function in preserving our institutions and our liberties. That this view has not always been acquiesced in by the legislative branch the following testifies:

"*Resolved*, That the judgment aforesaid is in its tendency, subversive of all law and order, and leads directly to anarchy and confusion; because if a court instituted for the benefit and government of a corporation may take upon them to dispense with an act in direct violation of a plain and known law of the state, all other courts, either superior or inferior may do the like; and therewith will end all our dear bought rights and privileges and legislatures become useless." Resolution of the Lower House of the New York Assembly after the decision in Rutgers *v*. Waddington, Journal of the New York Assembly, 1782 page 32. See *supra*, p. 18.

Probably the best comment on this are the remarks of the same court, or the justices of the court, on the same subject:

> It is but a decent respect due to the wisdom, the integrity, and the patriotism of the legislative body, by which any law is passed, to presume in favor of its validity, until its violation of the constitution is proved beyond all reasonable doubt. This has always been the language of this court, when that subject has called for its decision; and I know that it expresses the honest sentiments of each and every member of this bench.[1]
>
> This court can be insensible neither to the magnitude nor delicacy of this question. The validity of a legislative act is to be examined and the opinion of the highest law tribunal of a state is to be revised—an opinion which carries with it intrinsic evidence of the diligence, of the ability, and the integrity, with which it was formed. On more than one occasion, this court has expressed the cautious circumspection with which it approaches the consideration of such questions; and has declared, that in no doubtful case, would it pronounce a legislative act to be contrary to the constitution.[2]

It is apparent that whatever awe the Supreme Court of the United States ever had of the states has now quite completely disappeared. It no longer shows any per-

"The declaration by the people of Kentucky, that they *will be free*, would be superfluous; they cannot, until their habits and nature are changed, be otherwise; and they have no preference for *judicial tyranny*. They will not tolerate tyranny under any disguise; but while they abhor oppression under whatever mask, they love order, and will not violate it until no other alternative is left. Wherefore:

Resolved by the Legislature of the commonwealth of Kentucky, That they do hereby most solemnly protest, in the name and on the behalf of the good people of Kentucky, against the erroneous, injurious and degrading doctrines of the opinion of the Supreme Court of the United States, pronounced at the last session of that court, in the case of Green and Biddle." Kentucky Session Laws, 1823–24, p. 515.

[1] Ogden *v.* Saunders, 12 Wheat., 270, *supra*, p. 62.

[2] Dartmouth College *v.* Woodward, 4 Wheat., 625, *supra*, p. 59.

ceptible hesitancy when it concludes it must nullify an act of the state legislature. Instead of the great reluctance and regret with which the court formerly approached such a question now it approaches it with indifference or with the air of a superior about to discipline an inferior. If the court would exhibit more of its former respect for state statutes and show greater reluctance to interfere with the legislative body of the state, there would perhaps be less said about the interference of the federal judiciary in state affairs, and also the court would possibly be able to escape part of the criticism it now receives because of its alleged failure to interpret modern problems in the light of modern knowledge and necessity. If the Supreme Court is at liberty to nullify a state statute at its discretion, without awakening any great public clamor or criticism, is it to be considered remarkable that the court should, to some extent, substitute its own discretion for that of the state?

CHAPTER III

Analysis of the Federal Statutes Nullified by the Supreme Court of the United States.

Although the Supreme Court nullified a federal act very shortly after it was organized (Todd *v.* United States[1] in 1794), and its power to do so has not been seriously questioned since the decision of Marbury *v.* Madison[2] in 1803, yet a study of these cases shows that the Supreme Court has used this power rather sparingly so far as federal statutes are concerned. In almost a century and a quarter the Supreme Court has declared invalid in whole or in part because of constitutional conflict thirty-three United States statutes.[3] So far as quantity is concerned, therefore, it can scarcely be contended that the court has been intemperate in the use of this power in respect to federal statutes. But of course quantity is not the only or the main criterion by which to judge of the manner in which the court has used its authority. Another factor to be considered is obviously the character of the statutes annulled. Have these been of great and far-reaching importance, and have the decisions been of such a nature as to preclude the federal government from solving properly those numerous and important social and economic problems which have come into existence since the adoption of the constitution, are the real questions to be considered.

[1] 13 Howard, 52. [2] 1 Cranch, 137.

[3] See Appendix I for list of cases.

The cases in which statutes have been declared invalid group themselves more or less readily into four classes according to the constitutional character of the acts which have been declared void. In making this classification, however, absolute exactness is not claimed since it is quite possible that a statute may violate more than one provision of the constitution; also in this grouping the element of convenience of discussion has been considered. These four classes are as follows:

1. Laws disturbing the constitutional position of the three branches of the federal government.

2. Laws disturbing the federal relation and encroaching upon the powers of the states.

3. Laws trespassing upon the individual civil rights guaranteed by the constitution.

4. Other statutes not included in any of the above.

Section 1.—Laws disturbing the constitutional position of the three branches of the federal government:

13	How.,	52,	United States *v.* Todd, 1794.
1	Cranch,	137,	Marbury *v.* Madison, 1803.
2	Wall.,	561,	Gordon *v.* United States, 1864.
3	Wall.,	571,	The Alicia, 1868.
13	Wall.,	128,	United States *v.* Klein, 1871.
213	U. S.,	297,	United States *v.* Evans, 1908.
219	U. S.,	346,	Muskrat *v.* United States, 1910.

The first time that the justices of the Supreme Court expressed their opinion on the power of the court to nullify a statute because of constitutional conflict was in Hayburn's Case.[1] As previously indicated, this case was never decided by the Supreme Court though the justices expressed their opinions while on circuit. The statute which brought about a protest by the justices in this in-

[1] 2 Dallas 409, *supra* p. 37.

stance was an act which they thought assigned to them duties not judicial in nature, and which therefore encroached upon the independence of the judiciary.

The first case in which an act of Congress was apparently declared unconstitutional and hence void by the Supreme Court was United States *v.* Todd.[1] In this case almost the same question was presented and the principle involved was identical with that of the preceding case, as Congress had, according to the opinion of the court, attempted to encroach upon the judiciary by assigning administrative duties to the justices.

In the case which decided for all time the power of the Supreme Court to declare an act of Congress in conflict with the constitution and hence void, Marbury *v.* Madison,[2] a similar principle was involved though the facts are different. Congress had authorized the Supreme Court to issue the writ of mandamus in its original jurisdiction in a class of cases not mentioned in the constitution, and it was this statute which was passed upon in the famous decision. It was this that gave Chief Justice Marshall an opportunity to deliver his epoch-making opinion, as the decision held that the original jurisdiction of the Supreme Court was defined by the constitution and that Congress could neither add to nor subtract therefrom. Thus this great case, however far-reaching the reasoning may be, was in essence only another attempt of the judiciary to maintain its independence and prevent legislative encroachment.

The next case but one in which the court felt called upon to exercise again its power of vitiating a federal statute was Gordon *v.* United States.[3] Congress had created a Court of Claims and provided for an appeal

[1] 13 How. 52, *supra* p. 40.
[2] 1 Cranch 137, *supra* p. 42.
[3] 2 Wall., 561, and 117 U. S., 697.

from this tribunal to the Supreme Court under certain restrictions. One section of the act provided that no money should be paid out for any claim passed upon by the Court of Claims until after an appropriation had been estimated by the Secretary of the Treasury. Under this statute, as construed by the Supreme Court, neither that tribunal nor the Court of Claims could do anything more than certify their opinions to the Secretary of the Treasury and the latter might or might not include the amount awarded in his estimates and Congress might or might not appropriate the necessary funds. Neither court could, by any process, enforce its judgment and whether a claim adjudged to be due was paid did not depend upon the decisions of the courts but upon the discretion of the Secretary of the Treasury and Congress. The Supreme Court held that so far as it was concerned such provisions were impossible; that the Supreme Court was one of the co-ordinate branches of the government and that there was no constitutional power in Congress or elsewhere to supervise its judgment. It therefore refused to take jurisdiction in cases arising under the statute and declared void the part of the act attempting to confer such jurisdiction.

The next year the court again refused to accept jurisdiction which Congress attempted to bestow upon it. By statutes passed in 1863 and 1864, regarding the decision of prize cases arising from the Southern blockade, it was provided that such cases might be appealed directly from the federal District Courts to the Supreme Court; also that any such cases then pending in the Circuit Courts might, upon the application of all parties interested, be transferred to the Supreme Court. It was this last clause that was passed upon in The Alicia.[1]

[1] 7 Wall., 571.

This case had originally been heard in the District Court and then appealed to the Circuit Court before the above statute was enacted. Before the latter tribunal had heard the case, following the statute, an attempt was made to appeal to the Supreme Court, which held that since the decree of the lower court had been vacated by the appeal to the Circuit Court, there was no decree or judgment on which the Supreme Court might act, and hence that a hearing of the case would be in reality an exercise of original jurisdiction, while the constitution allowed only appellate authority in such instances. The court stated,

We are obliged to conclude that, in the provision for transfer, an attempt was inadvertently made to give to this court a jurisdiction withheld by the Constitution, and, consequently, that the order of transfer was without effect. The cause is still pending in the Circuit Court.

During the stress and turmoil resulting from the Civil War, Congress exceeded its power and encroached upon the spheres of both the executive and the judiciary according to the interpretation of the court.[1] The national legislature had provided that the government would reimburse owners for certain classes of property lost or abandoned during the war, provided the owner had given no aid to the rebellion, and recovery was to be made by suit in the Court of Claims with appeal to the Supreme Court. In a rider attached to an appropriation bill in 1870,[2] Congress enacted in substance that

[1] United States *v.* Klein, 13 Wall., 128.

[2] 16 Stat. at Large, 235. This statute was presumably passed to prevent the court from following the doctrine laid down in United States *v.* Padelford, 9 Wall., 531, which had been decided about two months before the act was passed. In this case the court had held that any one who had taken the oath of allegiance as provided by statute and executive proclamation for those who had engaged in the Southern rebellion,

no pardon or amnesty granted by the President should be admitted as evidence to support any claim against the United States or to establish the claimant's right to bring such suit, but the proof of loyalty must be made irrespective of any executive action, and this is "hereby declared to have been and to be the true intent and meaning of said respective acts" [Captured and Abandoned Property Acts]. It was also provided that if the Court of Claims had, after admission of such evidence, awarded judgment in favor of any claimant, the Supreme Court on appeal should have no further jurisdiction and should dismiss the case.

The court maintained that this involved the principle of separation of powers saying, "it is of vital importance that these powers be kept distinct." The statute, as construed, also impaired the effect of a pardon and thus infringed upon the constitutional power of the executive. The court, however, objected more strenously to what it considered an attempt by Congress to prescribe rules of decision for the judicial department, and to determine the decision of a judicial cause in a particular way, and denied that the statute was within the acknowledged power of Congress to make exceptions to, and prescribe regulations for, the appellate power of the court. The act was, therefore, declared inoperative.

In legislating for the District of Columbia Congress provided that,

In all criminal prosecutions the United States or the Dis-

was in the eye of the law "as innocent as if he had never committed the offense." By this interpretation of the Captured and Abandoned Property Act certain persons, provided they had taken the oath of allegiance, were enabled to sue the United States government for property lost during the Civil War, though such persons had voluntarily given aid to the enemy. Naturally the later attempt of Congress to control the court's decision was irritating to the latter.

trict of Columbia, as the case may be, shall have the same right of appeal as is given to the defendant, including the right to a bill of exceptions; provided, that if on such appeal it shall be found that there was error in the rulings of the court during the trial, a verdict in favor of the defendant shall not be set aside.[1]

Under this statute an appellate court of the District of Columbia refused jurisdiction when an attempt was made to appeal a case, and the Supreme Court of the United States upheld this ruling.[2] The Supreme Court took the position that this was in reality but giving an opinion on questions of law which were not before it in a "case," and that while this duty was required of some state tribunals, "No such requirement obtains in Federal jurisprudence," and, "It was long ago held by this court, that the discharge of such a function was not an exercise of judicial power."

In Muskrat *v.* United States[3] a peculiar legislative act was under consideration. Congress provided that certain Cherokee Indian claimants indicated by name, might, on their own behalf or on the behalf of others similarly situated, institute suit in the Court of Claims with the right of appeal to the Supreme Court to determine the validity of any acts of Congress passed since 1902, affecting the allotment of Cherokee lands. The Attorney General of the United States was authorized to defend such suits and other attorney fees, under certain contingencies, were to be determined by the court giving final judgment and to be paid out of funds in the possession of the United States government but belonging to the beneficiaries under the statutes indicated. The

[1] 31 Statutes at Large, 1341.

[2] United States *v.* Evans, 213 U. S, 297.

[3] 219 U. S., 346.

court declared that although the United States was made technically a party to the suit it had no interest adverse to the claimants; that Congress was making an attempt to obtain a judicial declaration of the validity of a statute though the question was not presented in the form of a "case" or "controversy" to which the judicial power constitutionally extends; that the question was not presented in such a manner that a binding and conclusive judgment could be rendered. The court refused to take jurisdiction and declared the statute invalid.

It will thus be seen that in attempting to maintain the balance of power between the three great branches of government the court has shown no tendency, by declaring statutes invalid, to enlarge its own jurisdiction to any extent. Of the seven statutes nullified, in whole or in part, because of a violation of this principle, the court was not extending its jurisdiction beyond the limits defined by the offending statute but in each case, with but one exception, it was voluntarily limiting or refusing the jurisdiction which Congress was attempting to bestow upon it. The court has in only one instance declared invalid a statute attempting to limit its jurisdiction. In this instance[1] the cases which it included by this means were of a particular class, limited in number, and which from the circumstances would continually decrease. Hence it is quite safe to say that the Supreme Court of the United States has not extended its jurisdiction unduly by its power of nullifying statutes because of conflict with the principle under discussion, and whatever increase of jurisdiction it may have acquired has been obtained by other means.

Moreover it is worthy of note that all these statutes

[1] United States *v.* Klein, *supra* p. 81.

referred to the judiciary alone, and in no instance was a federal act nullified because of an alleged attempt to bestow judicial powers on other branches of the government. While it is axiomatic in this country that no branch of the government may exercise judicial powers except the judiciary, yet with the growing complexity of the government it has been recognized that power very closely allied to the judicial must be exercised by the administration if the latter is not to be hampered in its legitimate work. With the tendency of Congress to bestow more and more of this quasi-judicial authority on administrative officials, the court has not interfered by its power to declare statutes unconstitutional. In all cases in which the court has nullified a statute because of conflict with the constitutional separation of powers it has done so in order to defend its own independence and, with one not important exception, it has uniformly limited its own authority. Also it is worthy of note that in two of the three instances in which the court nullified a federal statute up to 1866, it was simply protecting its own jurisdiction and in no way interfering with the general activities of Congress.

Section 2.—Statutes disturbing federal relations and encroaching upon the powers of the states:

9 Wall., 41, United States *v.* Dewitt, 1869.
11 Wall., 113, The Collectors *v.* Day, 1870.
17 Wall., 322, United States *v.* The Railroad Co., 1872.
92 U. S., 214, United States *v.* Reese, 1875.
95 U. S., 670, United States *v.* Fox, 1877.
100 U. S., 82, Trade Mark Cases, 1879.
106 U. S., 629, United States *v.* Harris, 1882.
109 U. S., 3, Civil Rights Cases, 1883.

120 U. S., 678, Baldwin *v.* Franks, 1886.
190 U. S., 127, James *v.* Bowman, 1903.
207 U. S., 463, Employers' Liability Cases, 1907.
213 U. S., 138, Keller *v.* United States, 1908.

In this class of cases there is frequently no specific clause of the constitution on which the court can base its decision but in a federal form of government, obviously, both the state and national governments must exist; also it is insisted that each must have its own sphere of activities and neither can trespass upon that of the other, for if these conditions are not maintained the federal scheme will be transformed into a unitary government or be dissolved into its component states. The Supreme Court has frequently held,[1] that owing to the inherent characteristics of the federal form of government and also to the fact that the constitution provides that the United States has only delegated powers, and powers not delegated to the United States government are reserved to the people or to the states,[2] that statutes, either state or national, which impair this balance of the two governments, are improper and cannot exist even though there is no specific clause of the Constitution violated.

The first case in which the Supreme Court decided that a federal statute conflicted with the principle mentioned above was United States *v.* DeWitt.[3] In the Internal Revenue Act of 1867, Congress forbade the sale of certain inflammable illuminating oils. The court in a short opinion held this was improper; that this was

[1] In addition to the cases discussed in this chapter, see e. g. Dobbins *v.* Commissioners, 16 Peters, 435; McCulloch *v.* Maryland, 4 Wheat., 316; Weston *v.* Charleston, 2 Peters, 449; Lane County *v.* Oregon, 7 Wall., 71.

[2] 10th Amendment.

[3] 9 Wall., 41.

purely a police regulation, and in attempting such regulations Congress was encroaching upon the police power vested in the states.

Another case in which the court had to pass upon the question of federal relations because of a national statute was Collector *v.* Day.[1] In certain laws passed between 1864 and 1867 Congress had provided that,

> There shall be levied, collected, and paid annually upon the gains, profits, and incomes of every person residing in the United States . . . . whether derived from any kind of property, rents, interests, dividends, or salaries, or from any profession, trade, employment or vocation, carried on in the United States or elsewhere, or from any other source whatever, a tax of 5 *per centum* on the amount so derived, over $1000.

With this statute on the books an attempt was made to collect the tax on the salary of a Massachusetts judge. The court held the enactment to be inoperative as applied to the salaries of state officials; that it was intended by the constitution to maintain the integrity of both the state and national governments and neither could infringe upon the legitimate powers of the other; and that taxing the salary of an officer of one government by the other was an interference which could not be tolerated.

Two years after the above case was decided the court again found it necessary to restrict the money-raising activities of Congress because of an encroachment upon the sphere of the state.[2] As one of its war measures

[1] 11 Wall., 113. This is the reverse side of the question decided in Dobbins *v.* Commissioners, 16 Peters, 435. In this latter instance the court had prevented the state from levying a tax on a federal officer as such.

[2] United States *v.* Railroad Co., 17 Wall., 322.

Congress had provided that the bond interest and dividends of all transportation companies should be taxed, the companies themselves deducting the tax from such interest or dividends and paying it into the United States treasury. Prior to this time the city of Baltimore had issued bonds and used the proceeds to aid in the construction of a railroad, the road giving the city a mortgage on its property. United States officials attempted to collect the tax on the mortgage interest payable to the city. The court held that the municipal corporation was so much a part of the state that its acts were the same as the acts of the state itself so far as the federal government was concerned. As the city had acted entirely for the public good and not in its private capacity, the income of the city could no more be taxed than could that of the state and the statute was to this extent invalid.[1]

In 1870 Congress passed a rather sweeping act,[2] supposedly based on the recently adopted fifteenth amendment, in regard to the right to vote. Portions of the act recognized the fact that this amendment applies only to cases of disfranchisement on account of race, color or previous condition of servitude, but other parts, as construed by the court, went beyond this and attempted to guarantee suffrage to citizens generally and provided penalties for any who should attempt to interfere with this right. The court held in United States *v.* Reese[3] that this was not "appropriate legislation" under the fifteenth amendment. It was maintained that the United States had but narrow power under this amendment, and that plainly it is only when the states refuse

[1] For a later interpretation of this principle, see South Carolina *v.* United States, 199 U. S., 437, *infra* note, p. 99.

[2] 16 Statutes at Large, 140.

[3] 92 U. S., 214.

a citizen a right to vote because of race, color or previous condition of servitude that Congress may appropriately act; that any legislation beyond this regulates local elections in excess of the powers of Congress; hence the act was held to be *ultra vires* and an encroachment upon the powers of the states.

In the supposed exercise of its power over bankruptcy the national legislature provided for the criminal punishment of any one who, within three months before bankruptcy proceedings were commenced, had obtained goods with the intent to defraud. The court,[1] while recognizing that Congress had power to enact any legislation necessary to execute its constitutional authority, yet held that,

> an act committed within a state, whether for a good or bad purpose, or whether with an honest or criminal intent, cannot be made an offense against the United States, unless it have some relation to the execution of a power of Congress, or to some matter within the jurisdiction of the United States. An act not having any such a relation is one in respect to which the state alone can legislate.
>
> The act described . . . is one which concerns only the State in which it is committed: it does not concern the United States.

The act consequently was of no force or effect.

Congress inspired presumably either because of its power to provide for the issuance of copyrights and patents or because of its control over interstate commerce, in two acts of 1870 and 1876, forbidding any counterfeiting or use of trademarks by others than the registered users, attempted to give to the latter about the same protection as the owner of a patent or copy-

[1] United States *v.* Fox, 95 U. S., 670.

right. The court held[1] that trademarks could not come under the patent or copyright powers of Congress; neither could the act be upheld because of the commerce clause since it was general in its terms and not limited to interstate or foreign commerce. Hence the statute was *ultra vires*, and an attempted use by Congress of power which belonged to the states since general control of property rights is vested in the latter.

Congress again testing its powers under the recently adopted amendments, in 1871 passed an act providing that if two or more persons conspired to deprive any one or any class of persons of the equal protection of the law, they would be liable to criminal prosecution and punishment. Again the court objected in United States *v.* Harris,[2] and substantially repeating the opinion it had already expressed in other cases,[3] that the fifteenth amendment obviously applied only to those instances where the right to vote was denied because of race, color, or previous condition of servitude, and hence afforded no basis for the statute in question; that the fourteenth amendment provided only against state action and did not permit the United States to legislate regarding the action of individuals; that the thirteenth amendment prohibiting slavery did not warrant such an act; and finally that article iv, section 2, of the constitution guaranteeing the citizens of each state all the privileges and immunities of citizens of the several states is directed exclusively to state action. The court could find no constitutional basis for the statute in question, and it was accordingly declared invalid.

Another result of the reconstruction and the newly

[1] Trade Mark Cases, 100 U. S., 82.

[2] 106 U. S., 629.

[3] See *e. g.* U. S. *v.* Reese, 92 U. S., 214, *supra*, p. 88; U. S. *v.* Cruikshank, 92 U. S., 542; Paul *v.* Virginia, 8 Wall., 168.

adopted amendments was an act of Congress attempting to guarantee to all equal rights and accommodations in public conveyances and places of public amusement or entertainment, and this act was to be "applicable alike to citizens of every race and color, regardless of any previous condition of servitude." Several prosecutions arose under this act and were heard together under the title of the Civil Rights Cases.[1] The court discussed fully the fourteenth amendment and the power which Congress has under it. On this point the court states:

It is state action of a particular character that is prohibited [by the amendment]. Individual invasion of individual rights is not the subject matter of the amendment. It has a deeper and broader scope. It nullifies and makes void all State legislation, and State action of every kind, which impairs the privileges and immunities of citizens of the United States, or which injures them in life, liberty or property without due process of law, or which denies to any of them the equal protection of the laws. It not only does this, but, in order that the national will, thus declared, may not be a mere *brutum fulmen*, the last section of the amendment invests Congress with the power to enforce it by appropriate legislation. To enforce what? To enforce the prohibition. To adopt appropriate legislation for correcting the effects of such prohibited State laws and State acts, and thus to render them effectually null, void, and innocuous. This is the legislative power conferred upon Congress, and this is the whole of it. It does not invest Congress with power to legislate upon subjects which are within the domain of State legislation; but to provide modes of relief against State legislation, or State action, of the kind referred to.[2]

[1] 109 U. S., 3. *Cf.* Slaughter House Cases, 16 Wall., 36, 1872, in which the court first gave a general review of the newly adopted amendments.

[2] Also the thirteenth amendment was considered and the court held that mere discrimination in public places was not slavery nor any servitude prohibited by the thirteenth amendment.

The power which Congress has to pass appropriate legislation thus extends only to corrective legislation, *i. e.*, in effect Congress may simply provide proper modes of appeal from the state to the federal courts and cannot itself aid any one who has been denied the rights guaranteed by the fourteenth amendment. By this interpretation the court drew into its own hands the entire effective power which was given the federal government by this amendment. It is to determine if the states have, by any official act, violated the provisions of the amendment. The court secured no positive authority over the states, but it does have large negative power by virtue of its authority to determine what they may not do, but Congress was left with neither positive nor negative power. It is true that the court before this had exercised considerable control over the states largely because of the commerce and obligation of contract clauses[1] of the constitution, but by thus interpreting the fourteenth amendment it vastly increased its influence over the states. This control was still further augmented when the amendment was turned from its original purpose to shield the negro race,[2] and used to

[1] Art. I, sections 8 and 10. See Appendix V for list of cases in which state statutes have been nullified by the Supreme Court of the United States because of conflict with these clauses.

[2] *Cf.* "On the most casual examination of the language of these amendments, no one can fail to be impressed with the one prevailing purpose found in them all, lying at the foundation of each, and without which none of them would have been even suggested; we mean the freedom of the slave race, the security and firm establishment of that freedom, and the protection of the newly made freeman and citizen from the oppressions of those who had formerly exercised unlimited dominion over him. It is true that only the fifteenth amendment, in terms, mentions the negro by speaking of his color and his slavery. But it is just as true that each of the other articles was addressed to the grievances of that race, and designed to remedy them as the fifteenth.

protect property rights. In the case under discussion the court by denying to Congress any positive power and indicating the matter in which the provisions of the fourteenth amendment were to be executed, very greatly increased the influence of the judiciary, and this too at the expense of a co-ordinate branch of the government.[1]

"We do not say that no one else but the negro can share in this protection. Both the language and the spirit of these articles are to have their fair and just weight in any question of construction. Undoubtedly while negro slavery alone was in the mind of Congress which proposed the thirteenth article, it forbids any other kind of slavery, now or hereafter. If Mexican peonage or the Chinese coolie labor system shall develop slavery of the Mexican or Chinese race within our territory, this amendment may be safely trusted to make it void. And so if other rights are assailed by the States which properly and necessarily fall within the protection of these articles, that protection will apply, though the party interested may not be of African descent. But what we do say, and what we wish to be understood is, that in any fair and just construction of any section or phrase of these amendments, it is necessary to look to the purpose which we have said was the prevailing spirit of them all, the evil which they were designed to remedy, and the process of continued addition to the Constitution, until that purpose was supposed to be accomplished, as far as constitutional law can accomplish it." Slaughter House Cases, 16 Wall., 36, 71.

[1] A justice of the court thus expresses his opinion of this decision: "This court has always given a broad and liberal construction to the constitution, so as to enable Congress, by legislation, to enforce rights secured by that instrument. The legislation which Congress may enact, in execution of its power to enforce the provisions of this amendment, is such as may be appropriate to protect the right granted. The word appropriate was undoubtedly used with reference to its meaning, as established by repeated decisions of this court. Under given circumstances, that which the court characterizes as corrective legislation might be deemed by Congress appropriate and entirely sufficient. Under other circumstances primary direct legislation may be required. But it is for Congress, not the judiciary, to say what legislation is appropriate—that is—best adapted to the end to be attained. The judiciary may not, with safety to our institutions, enter the domain of legislative discretion, and dictate the means which Congress shall employ in the exercise of its granted powers. That would be sheer usurpation of the functions of a coördinate department, which, if often repeated, and per-

The last case[1] in which an act of Congress supposedly based on the fifteenth amendment was declared unconstitutional was James *v.* Bowman,[2] in 1902, though the statute in question was passed in 1870. One section of the act forbade interference by threats or bribery with any one exercising, or attempting to exercise, the right to vote to whom that right was guaranteed by the fifteenth amendment. The court held that Congress had exceeded its powers, inasmuch as the statute was aimed at the acts of the individual and the court had already objected to this;[3] neither could the act be upheld because of the control which Congress has over certain elections, as the act applied to all elections, and "Congress has no power to punish bribery at all elections. The limits of its powers are in respect to elections in which the nation is directly interested, or in which some mandate of the National Constitution is disobeyed," and the court refused to limit a statute general in its terms to those particulars which Congress could constitutionally regulate.

The cases immediately preceding grew out of statutes passed during the Civil War and its aftermath, the period

manently acquiesced in, would work a radical change in our system of government." Dissenting opinion of Justice Harlan, Civil Rights Cases, 109 U. S., 50.

[1] In Baldwin *v.* Franks, 120 U. S., 678, the constitutional validity of the same statute which was passed upon and found wanting in United States *v.* Harris (*supra*, p. 90) was again considered. The facts in the two cases differed. In the Harris case the conspiracy forbidden by the statute was alleged to have been formed by citizens of the United States against other citizens. In Baldwin *v.* Franks the alleged conspiracy was against alien Chinese, and it was contended that while the statute was inoperative in the first case it might be valid in the second. The court held to its previous decision that the statute was void within a state regardless of particular facts.

[2] 190 U. S., 127.

[3] See *e. g.*, Civil Rights Cases, *supra*, p. 91.

of Reconstruction. The next case chronologically in this class, however, deals with an entirely new subject—an attempt on the part of Congress to solve one of the more pressing industrial problems of the day, and the attempt was checked to some extent by the court in the Employers' Liability Cases.[1] The Congressional act[2] provided that every common carrier engaged in trade in the District of Columbia, in the territories or in interstate or foreign traffic was liable to its employees for any injuries to them because of negligence of the company's officers or employees or because of defective appliances or machinery. Not only did the act thus abrogate the fellow-servant rule of the common law but it also in another section rendered less harsh the doctrine of contributory negligence. When the question of the validity of this statute was presented to the court five separate opinions were handed down, and as a result it is somewhat difficult to say by an examination of the case exactly what was decided. However, by the concurrence of five of the justices the act was declared unconstitutional because it was general in its terms, including intrastate as well as interstate commerce, and hence was *ultra vires* and void. The opinion of the court, entirely concurred in by only one justice other than the writer of it, held that Congress had power to pass such an act provided it was limited to interstate commerce. Three of the justices, while concurring in the opinion that the statute was unconstitutional for the reasons stated, did not agree with all that part of the opinion which held that Congress could regulate the relations between employer and employee even when both were engaged in interstate commerce. Three of the four dissenting justices expressly affirmed the

[1] 207 U. S., 463.

[2] 32 Statutes at Large, 232.

power of Congress to pass acts regulating the relations between employer and employee engaged in interstate commerce, and the fourth dissenting justice impliedly gave his assent to this doctrine, since he held that it was possible to so interpret the present statute as to make it constitutional. In other words, in dealing with one of the more pressing industrial problems the court struck a compromise. It was willing, as indicated by the individual expressions of the justices, to allow Congress to legislate regarding the relations between employee and employer, and abrogate some of the outgrown common-law doctrines, so far as these employees were engaged solely in interstate commerce. When, however, it came to intrastate traffic, even though that traffic might be conducted by companies which also did interstate commerce, it held to the old doctrine that this is purely a state matter, and hence beyond the power of Congress to regulate. Three of the justices, however, refused to agree with the court that Congress could regulate the relations between employee and employer even in interstate commerce.[1]

[1] Congress almost immediately embodied the essential features of this act in another statute but limiting its application to interstate commerce by railroad and to railroad common carriers generally in the territories and possessions (35 Stat. at Large, 65, and 36 Stat. at Large, 291). The statute thus amended was reviewed by the court in the Second Employers' Liability Cases, 223 U. S., 1. The court, holding to the opinion of the majority of the justices in the previous Liability Cases, stated "that Congress, in the exertion of its power over interstate commerce, may regulate the relations of common carriers by railroad and their employees, while both are engaged in such commerce, subject always to the limitations prescribed in the Constitution, and to the qualification that the particulars in which those relations are regulated must have a real or substantial connection with the interstate commerce in which the carriers and their employees are engaged." The ccurt then considered other objections argued against the statute, mostly of a minor nature, and upheld the act.

In Keller *v.* United States[1] the national government was attempting to deal with an old evil, but by the more effective means demanded by a newly-awakened consciousness of the extent and viciousness of the evil. Congress in seeking some remedy for the "white slave" traffic provided that any one who was in any way instrumental in the importation of women for immoral purposes was guilty of a felony; the same act also provided that any one who harbored, for immoral purposes, any alien woman within three years from the time she entered the country, was likewise guilty of felony. It was this latter part of the statute that was attacked as unconstitutional. The court, while again affirming the power of Congress to exclude aliens, to prescribe the terms on which they might enter the country or to provide for their deportation, held that Congress had overstepped its constitutional limits in this instance.

While the keeping of a house of ill-fame is offensive to the moral sense, yet that fact must not close the eye to the question whether the power to punish therefor is delegated to Congress or is reserved to the State. Jurisdiction over such an offense comes within the accepted definition of the police power. Speaking generally, that power is reserved to the States, for there is in the Constitution no grant thereof to Congress.

The court held that this was not legislation respecting the conduct of an alien while domiciled in this country, nor was it respecting any wrong done such a person as no wrong was alleged, but the act attempted to control generally the dealings of citizens with aliens. The opinion declared if this was permitted,

[1] 213 U. S., 138.

We should be brought face to face with such a change in the internal conditions of this country as was never dreamed of by the framers of the Constitution. While the acts of Congress are to be liberally construed in order to enable it to carry into effect the powers conferred, it is equally true that prohibitions and limitations upon those powers should also be fairly and reasonably enforced. To exaggerate in the one direction and restrict in the other will tend to substitute one consolidated government for the present Federal system. We should never forget . . . that "the Constitution, in all its provisions, looks to an indestructible Union, composed of indestructible States."

Hence the part of the act under consideration was declared without constitutional basis and consequently void. By this decision the country was denied the right to take one of the most effective measures which the national government might have adopted to wipe out this ancient and vicious evil,—and the matter left largely to the care or the indifference of forty-eight separate states.

In the above an attempt has been made to analyze the statutes which have been annulled because of federal enroachment upon the powers of the states, for the purpose of indicating the extent to which this principle has been used to nullify statutes and also to show the importance of the statutes thus destroyed. It remains now to summarize as far as possible the results of the above analysis and ascertain what effect the enforcement of the federal principle, as interpreted by the court, has had on national legislation.

It is worthy of note that the court did not overturn a statute because of this principle until 1869 and thus up till after the Civil War, Congress was in no way hampered by judicial nullifications along this line. Also, as might be expected, the greater number of cases nullified because of conflict with this principle were decided in the decade 1865–1875 when the statutes passed by a partisan Congress as a result of the War had had time to work through the lower tribunals and reach the Supreme Court for final determination. During the decade 1890–1900 there were no statutes nullified at all because of this principle, but three were nullified during the following ten years though the statute in one case[1] dates back to 1870 and hence really belongs to the first decade mentioned. Two of the cases deal with an interference with the machinery of government, The Collector *v.* Day[2] and United States *v.* The Railroad Co.,[3] the court in both cases refusing to allow the national government to interfere, by taxation, with the officers or public income of the state or of its creatures. As it is elemental that the power to tax is the power to destroy the court was clearly within a safe principle when it refused to allow either[4] government to interfere with the public income or payments of the other.[5] The only question that can occur here then is

[1] James *v.* Bowman, 190 U. S., 127, *supra*, p. 94.

[2] *Supra*, p. 87.

[3] *Supra*, p. 87.

[4] *Cf.* Dobbins *v.* The Commissioners, 16 Peters, 435.

[5] Another decision regarding the relative financial powers of the two governments was rendered in South Carolina *v.* United States, 199 U. S., 437. Under what was known as the Dispensary Act, the state of South Carolina had direct control of the sale of intoxicating liquor within its borders, and since it was thus a state matter a protest was made against the payment of the federal internal revenue duties. In its decision the court pointed out the effect which state or municipal socialism might have on the federal income if the tax in this case was not valid, for by a state monopoly of federal-taxed articles the state might wholly avoid any national taxes. The tax in this case was upheld because by going into the liquor business the state laid aside its "sovereign" character and acted as an ordinary private corporation. "It is reasonable to hold that while the former [United States] may do noth-

one of application of the principle. In Collector *v.* Day the court was protecting the salary of a state officer from direct taxation by the national government and probably no one will criticise the court for its decision.[1] The United States *v.* The Railroad Co., was simply a limited application of the principle to a class of cases which is not likely to be either numerous or important. Hence there can be no just criticism of the court because of an undue interference with Congressional activities in this case.

The court gave the fifteenth amendment a narrow interpretation and as a result in two cases, United States *v.* Reese[2] and James *v.* Bowman,[3] statutes supposedly based on this amendment were declared void. This may perhaps be unfortunate but the unfortunate part was probably not the decision of the court but the conditions prevailing in certain sections of the country. However much it is to be deplored that in a democratic country there is a politically disqualified class, this regret does not change the fact that in the decade, 1865–1875, when this legislation was passed, there was a class incapable of taking its place politically with the white inhabitants. Congress was apparently obsessed with the idea that a race could be given equality by mere legislation, regardless of the qualifications of that race, or regardless of public sentiment, and attempted to secure that equality. The Supreme Court, while not checking the legislation so long as it remained within the strict letter of the amendment,

ing by taxation in any form to prevent the full discharge by the latter [the state] of its governmental functions, yet whenever a state engages in a business which is of a private nature that business is not withdrawn from the taxing power of the Nation."

[1] Two justices, however, dissented from the opinion of the court in this case.

[2] *Supra*, p. 88.

[3] *Supra*, p. 94.

refused any broad interpretation, and the spirit was not, in fact, much considered. Since the attempt by the national government to compel political equality for the colored race has been practically abandoned, and the states by various ingenious methods, allowed to control the question of voting to a very large extent, these cases are now largely of historical rather than of present or future interest. Also, considering conditions, probably few or none will now censure the court for its opinions in these cases. Congress attempted what later events demonstrated to be impossible and the court showed no great willingness to aid it in its attempt.

In regard to the court's interpretations of the fourteenth amendment it is exceedingly doubtful if so kindly a criticism can be made. By its power to render void an act of Congress the court has greatly increased its own jurisdiction and its control over legislative discretion. The cases along this line have, however, been already commented on.[1]

The statute which was tested and found wanting in United States *v.* DeWitt[2] was a clear exercise of the police power of the sort which the states ought to be capable of handling themselves since it involved no questions like inter-state commerce which are at times difficult for the states to deal with satisfactorily because of United States constitutional complications. Likewise the statute considered in United States *v.* Fox[3] was an attempt to provide for the punishment of an ordinary crime which the states can attend to without difficulty, and the act nullified in the Trade Mark Cases[4] is one affecting property rights, general control of which belongs to the states.

[1] *Supra*, p. 91 *et seq.*

[2] *Supra*, p. 86.

[3] *Supra*, p. 89.

[4] *Supra*, p. 90.

According to the doctrine held from the beginning of constitutional government in this country, that in general the states have a monopoly of the police power and the authority to regulate property rights, and considering the nature of the statutes involved in these cases, no criticism can be made of the court because of the use of its power to nullify statutes in these instances. But may the same be said of the decisions in the Employers Liability Cases[1] and of Keller *v.* United States?[2] Here Congress was attempting to deal with either a recent, or a new view of an ancient, evil, in both cases important questions, and in both cases Congress met with a partial check because the Supreme Court declared the statutes unconstitutional in whole or in part.

From the above it is seemingly safe to conclude that in exercising its power to nullify a federal statute because it encroaches upon the sphere of the state, as the Supreme Court interprets this, the court, in a majority of cases has used its power in such a manner as to subject it to no great amount of hostile criticism. Some of the statutes dealt with in cases coming under this heading, were clear infringements upon the powers of the states and others dealt with attempts of Congress to settle a racial question by means more than doubtful if judged by their effectiveness. But on the other hand the court has used its great power to produce two other results: (1) It has greatly increased its own authority and jurisdiction under the fourteenth amendment; (2) it has hampered Congress in its attempts to solve two pressing economic and social problems. The first has already been discussed. The second will be taken up later.

[1] *Supra*, p. 95.

[2] *Supra*, p. 97.

Section III.—Cases in which statutes were nullified because of encroachments upon individual civil rights.

4 Wall., 333, *Ex parte* Garland, 1866.
6 Wall., 160, Reichart *v.* Felps, 1867.
9 Wall., 274, The Justices *v.* Murray, 1869.
116 U. S., 616, Boyd *v.* United States, 1885.
127 U. S., 540, Callan *v.* Wilson, 1887.
142 U. S., 547, Counselman *v.* Hitchcock, 1891.
148 U. S., 312, Monongahela Navigation Co. *v.* United States, 1892.
163 U. S., 228, Wong Wing *v.* United States, 1895.
174 U. S., 47, Kirby *v.* United States, 1899.
[1] 197 U. S., 516, Rassmussen *v.* United States, 1905.
208 U. S., 161, Adair *v.* United States, 1907.

Although the courts from the very beginning of our government have declared themselves the special protectors of those fundamental personal rights claimed by all Englishmen and constitutionally guaranteed to American citizens, yet it was not until 1866 that the Supreme Court thought that Congress had trespassed upon any of those privileges, and then the transgression was the result of the bitterness and turmoil growing out of, and following, the Civil War.

In 1865 Congress provided that no attorney should be allowed to practice before a federal court unless he had first taken an oath that he had in no way voluntarily aided the Rebellion. The court in Ex parte Garland,[2] five justices agreeing, held that this action was improper, since it conflicted with the constitutional clauses prohibiting bills of attainder and ex-post-facto laws. Also since in the case at the bar, the individual con-

[1] In this case individual civil rights were of secondary rather than primary importance.

[2] 4 Wall., 333.

cerned had been pardoned by the President, Congress could not inflict any punishment which might not be relieved by executive clemency.[1]

Also during the stress of the Civil War, Congress enacted that if any suit was prosecuted, under certain circumstances, in any state court during the Rebellion against any officer of the United States, it would be competent for either party to remove the case any time within six months after the rendition of judgment, to the Circuit Court of the United States, "and the said Circuit Court shall thereupon proceed to try and determine the facts and law in such action, in the same manner as if the same had been there originally commenced, the judgment in such case notwithstanding."[2] It was alleged that this violated the second part of the seventh amendment providing that "No fact tried by a jury shall be otherwise re-examined in any court of the United States than according to the rules of the common law." The court held in the Justices *v.* Murray,[3] that this provision of the constitution applied to cases originating in the state courts and then carried to the federal courts as well as to actions originating in the latter, and to re-examine facts once determined by a jury in the manner contemplated by the statute was not the rule of com-

[1] The next case in chronological order is Reichart *v.* Felps, 6 Wall., 160. A statute of Congress passed in 1812 was reviewed and held inoperative in this instance. Congress by an act of 1788 had provided for the confirmation of certain land claims of settlers in the Northwest Territory. Later in 1812 a Board of Commissioners was authorized to revise and re-examine the confirmations made by the Governors of the Territory under the act of 1788. Two claimants appeared for certain land in Illinois—one claiming under the act of 1788 and the other under the act of 1812. The court in deciding the case stated that Congress had "no power to organize a board of revision to nullify titles confirmed many years before by the authorized agents of the government."

[2] 16 Statutes at Large, 757.

[3] 9 Wall., 274.

mon law. Hence the statute was null and void because of constitutional conflict.

The next case in which the court felt bound to annul an act of Congress because it violated the Bill of Rights was Boyd *v.* United States.[1] Congress had passed a rather drastic act[2] to aid in the collection of customs duties, empowering a court, in case the defendant importer had any paper, record, etc. which might be deemed of service to the government in the prosecution of a suit, to issue a notice to the defendant to produce such paper or record. If the defendant failed to comply with the order, the allegation made by the government, and which it expected to prove by the paper or record, should be taken as confessed. In words, criminal actions were specifically excluded from the operations of this act, and also no seizure or search was directly authorized. The court, however, claiming to look to the substance rather than the form of the statute, held that such a forced production of a man's private papers was equivalent to the search and seizure prohibited by the fourth amendment. It was also maintained that while in the case at trial the proceedings were in form civil they were in fact criminal, and consequently the act violated that part of the fifth amendment which prohibits any one being compelled to be a witness against himself in a criminal case. In this case while the court upheld the civil rights guaranteed by the constitution and its amendments, yet the act dealt only with the method used by the government in collecting its revenue. Because of the narrow application of both the statute and the decision,[3] no great significance can be attached to either.

[1] 116 U. S., 616.

[2] 18 Statutes at Large, 186.

[3] Some of the statements in this case are of a broad, general nature

In Callan *v.* Wilson,[1] there were two constitutional questions before the court for determination. One was whether the guarantees of personal rights and liberty apply to the District of Columbia and limit Congress in its legislation for the District. The court held the constitution did apply. The other point of general import was the determination of what is necessary in order to meet the constitutional requirement for trial by jury in criminal cases. Congress had provided for a summary trial in the District of Columbia Police Court in certain criminal cases, allowing an appeal to the court above provided the party applying for the appeal should give bond to appear and prosecute the case or that failing to give bond, he should remain in jail pending the decision in the appellate court. The court held that this procedure did not meet the requirements of the constitution; that with the exception of certain minor offenses which had always been tried with no jury at all, the constitution required a jury trial in the court of first instance, thus taking a broader view of the constitutional guarantees than Congress had taken and fulfilling the judicial claim that the courts are the best protectors of individual rights. Because of the fact that Congress has entire legislative control over very limited territory and because of the fact that it would probably never attempt any legislation similar to this for the guidance of the federal judiciary, due to the nature of the circumstances, this case, like the preceding, has no very wide direct signifi-

and not specifically limited to the point at issue. Since, however, it is a case in which the United States government appears because of its fiscal operations there may be doubt whether this language is really as broad as it appears or whether it must be limited in application to other cases similar in character to this one.

[1] 127 U. S., 540.

cance, though its indirect influence on state legislation and judicial decisions might be considerable.

In Counselman *v.* Hitchcock,[1] the court again passed upon a statute originally enacted in 1868, but re-enacted and included in the Interstate Commerce Act of 1887. The contest before the court grew out of an attempt to apply the statute in a railroad rebate case. Congress had provided that the courts could compel the officers and agents of carrier companies to appear and testify in certain cases, but that no evidence given by a party or a witness in a judicial proceeding should be used against that party or witness in any criminal proceedings in any court of the United States. In a grand jury investigation the government endeavored to obtain information from the plaintiff in the above case regarding alleged rebating in freight rates. The plaintiff refused to give the information asked for, claiming that notwithstanding the provision of the statute the fifth amendment still protected him. The court decided that the statute did not give the immunity required by the amendment and hence could not be enforced. While probably quite within the letter and spirit of the constitution this decision has embarrassed the government somewhat in dealing with corporations since, as it is obviously only through their officers that such organizations can be reached, and if these officers may not be compelled to testify regarding the doings of the corporations because of the possibility of personal prosecution, the difficulty of the government in controlling corporations is correspondingly increased. Thus, while the court was ostensibly upholding individual rights, corporations really

[1] 142 U. S., 547.

received the benefit of the court's solicitude for these personal privileges in this case.[1]

Because of the clause in the Bill of Rights, "Nor shall private property be taken for public use without just compensation," the court again protected property interests from Congressional aggression in Monongahela Navigation Co. *v.* United States.[2] The state of Pennsylvania had chartered the litigant company in this case and authorized it to construct improvements for the purpose of aiding commerce on a navigable river. Later, in 1881, Congress made an appropriation for the same purpose, the appropriation to be available only when the company had made certain additional improvements. The company met the requirements and in 1887 a second federal act was passed providing a certain amount for the purchase of these company improvements. The act also provided that, failing of purchase, the Secretary of War was to proceed to the condemnation of the property, but, "In estimating the sum to be paid by the United States, the franchise of said corporation to collect tolls shall not be considered or estimated." In the condemnation proceedings which succeeded, the company offered to prove among other things that twelve per

[1] This case was decided in January, 1892. In February, 1893, Congress, while still retaining the compulsory testifying clauses, so amended this section of the statute as to prohibit prosecution "for or on account of any transaction, matter or thing, concerning which he may testify, or produce evidence, . . ." 27 Statutes at Large, 443. In Brown *v.* Walker, 161 U. S., 591, this statute was held, four justices dissenting, to afford sufficient immunity, and a witness in these cases could not refuse to testify because of the fifth amendment. In a later case, Wilson *v.* United States, 221 U. S., 361, it was held that an officer of a corporation having possession of the books of the corporation must produce such books on proper judicial demand even though they might tend to incriminate the officer.

[2] 148 U. S., 312.

cent dividends had been paid on the stock and that the latter was worth about double the par value, but the lower court following the statute refused to admit any evidence of this character. On appeal, the Supreme Court stated that,

> Obviously, this question, as all others which run along the line of the extent of the protection the individual has under the Constitution against the demands of the government, is of importance; for in any society the fulness and sufficiency of the securities which surround the individual in the use and enjoyment of his property constitute one of the most certain tests of the character and value of the government.

The court then holds that the deprivation of the right to collect tolls, given to a company by a government, is as much a taking of property in the constitutional sense as is the confiscation of more tangible possessions and

> The question of just compensation is not determined by the value to the government which takes, but the value to the individual from whom the property is taken; and when by the taking of the tangible property the owner is actually deprived of the franchise to collect tolls, just compensation requires payment, not merely of the value of the tangible property itself, but also of that of the franchise of which he is deprived.

Hence the particular clause forbidding compensation for the franchise, which Congress had carefully inserted, was nullified. In this case the court proved itself a stouter defender of property rights than Congress but in so doing it made no mention of the fact that "just" compensation includes justice both to the individual and to society, and in this instance Congress had not attempted to take away without compensation any value which the company had given its property but only that contributed by the public. The statute would have returned this value to the community which created it without cost to the latter but the court refused to allow such restitution.[1]

The federal government had passed considerable legislation in regard to the Chinese, all of it hostile and some of it drastic. The court had allowed Congress full discretion in prohibiting the immigration of Chinese and providing for the deportation of those unlawfully within the country, as well as submitting the enforcement of such laws exclusively to the executive officers without judicial review.[2] When, however, in 1892[3] Congress provided that any Chinese person who was adjudged unlawfully within the United States by any justice, judge or commissioner of the United States should be imprisoned, prior to deportation, for a period not to exceed one year, the court called a halt. In Wong Wing *v.* United States[4] it was held that this section of the statute was contrary to the jury-trial provisions of the fifth and sixth amendments. Certainly the court in these Chinese immigration cases allowed Congress all the liberty that could reasonably be claimed and only checked it when both the letter and the spirit of the constitution were clearly violated.

In Kirby *v.* United States[5] the court nullified part of a federal act[6] affecting evidence in cases involving the

[1] As to whether the franchise should be included in the property on which a fair return must be allowed in fixing rates for public utilities, see *e. g.* Knoxville *v.* Water Co., 212 U. S., 1, and Willcox *v.* Gas Co., 212 U. S., 19.

[2] *Cf.* Chae Chan Ping *v.* United States, 130 U. S., 581; Fong Ting *v.* United States, 149 U. S., 698; Lem Moon Sing *v.* United States, 158 U. S., 538; see also United States *v.* Ju Toy, 198 U. S., 253.

[3] 27 Statutes at Large, 25.

[4] 163 U. S., 228.

[5] 174 U. S., 47.

[6] 18 Statutes at Large, 479.

misappropriation of United States government property or money. As the court construed this act it was in conflict with that clause of the sixth amendment which requires an accused in criminal prosecutions to be confronted with the witnesses against him. The statute in question dealt only with the attempt of the government to protect its own property and, at least so far as the particular points at issue are concerned, the case has but a narrow application without general importance.[1]

After the great railroad strikes of 1894, Congress set about devising means to lessen or prevent such catastrophes in the future, and embodied its conclusions in an act passed June, 1898. The act applied only to carriers engaged in interstate or foreign commerce with certain named exceptions, and provided for settlement, by means of arbitration, of controversies concerning wages, hours of labor, etc., and labor unions were to be recognized in forming the boards of conciliation. The act further provided that no employer nor any of his officers or agents should attempt to prevent employees from joining or remaining members of a labor union, nor "shall threaten any employee with loss of employment, or shall unjustly discriminate against any employee because of his membership in such a labor corporation, association, or organization."[2] This latter section of the statute was considered in Adair *v.* United States,[3] the specific question as the court defined it being:

[1] In Rassmussen *v.* United States, 197 U. S., 516, it was held that a statute providing for a jury of six men for the trial of certain offenses in Alaska, was invalid. The question really at issue in this case was, however, whether the constitution applied to Alaska, and limited Congress in its territorial legislation. The court held that the Constitution did apply and consequently only the common-law jury of twelve men could be utilized—a fact conceded by the government if the constitutional limitations extended to the territory.

[2] 30 Statutes at Large, 424.

[3] 208 U. S., 161.

May Congress make it a criminal offense against the United States—as by the tenth section of the act of 1898 it does—for an agent or officer of an interstate carrier, having full authority in the premises from the carrier, to discharge an employee from service simply because of his membership in a labor organization?

It was alleged that Congress derived constitutional power from the interstate commerce clause to pass such an act, but the court held,

that there is no such connection between interstate commerce and membership in a labor organization as to authorize Congress to make it a crime against the United States for an agent of an interstate carrier to discharge an employee because of such membership on his part.

Not only did the act have the negative defect of being unauthorized by the constitution, but it was positively bad because it conflicted with a specific provision of the constitution—the due process clause of the fifth amendment. The court held that an interference with a man's right to sell his labor or an employer's right to buy that labor, unless the interference was based on recognized police power, was in conflict with the "liberty" guaranteed by the due process clause. In this instance a part of the act was declared void, though as Mr. Justice Holmes says in his dissenting opinion, it was "a very limited interference with freedom of contract, no more." To quote the court:

In our opinion that section, in the particular mentioned, is an invasion of the personal liberty as well as of the right of property, guaranteed by that [fifth] amendment. Such liberty and right embraces the right to make contracts for the purchase of the labor of others and equally the right to make contracts for the sale of one's own labor; each right, however, being subject to the fundamental condition that no contract, whatever its subject matter, can be sustained which the law, upon reasonable grounds, forbids as inconsistent with the public interests or hurtful to the public order or as detrimental to the common good. . . . It is sufficient in this case to say that as agent of the railroad company and as such responsible for the conduct of the business of one of its departments, it was the defendant Adair's right—and that right inhered in his personal liberty, and was also a right of property—to serve his employer as best he could, so long as he did nothing that was reasonably forbidden by law as injurious to the public interests. It was the right of the defendant to prescribe the terms upon which the services of Coppage[1] would be accepted and it was the right of Coppage to become or not, as he chose, an employee of the railroad company upon the terms offered to him.

This is the second time that the due process clause has been used as a reason for nullifying an act of Congress. In the previous case of Hepburn *v.* Griswold,[2] this clause was only mentioned and not elaborated to any great extent, but in the present case it is one of two reasons for annulling an act of Congress. Perhaps it is only fair to raise the question whether the court in the future will develop the due process clause as applied to the federal government, as due process shows itself capable of development, and by this means control the discretion of Congress to the extent that the discretion of the state legislatures is now being controlled by virtue of the similar clause in the fourteenth amendment.[3]

[1] Coppage was the employee discharged in alleged violation of the act.

[2] 8 Wall, 603, *infra*, p. 118.

[3] One of the justices of the Supreme Court thus expresses himself regarding this decision: "It also seems to me to be an oversight of the proportions of things to contend that, in order to encourage a policy of arbitration between carriers and their employees which may prevent a dis-

From the above analysis it will be seen that Congress has shown no great tendency to violate any of the civil rights guaranteed by the constitution, and in no great number of cases has the Supreme Court had to interfere and check Congressional activity because of the Bill of Rights in the constitution; nor, judging again by the quantity of cases, has the court been unduly active in the exercise of its power to nullify statutes because of conflict with the constitutional civil guarantees. The court has used its powers to soften the drastic legislation excited by bitter partisan feeling,—popular agitation or resentment against certain classes. In *ex parte* Garland[1] the court refused to allow Congress to impose certain humiliations and oppressions upon a defeated people. Likewise in Wong Wing *v.* United States,[2] while the court had been very lenient, it did refuse to tolerate gross mistreatment of a disliked race.

astrous interruption of commerce, the derangement of business, and even greater evils to the public welfare, Congress cannot restrain the discharge of an employee and yet can, to enforce a policy of unrestrained competition between railroads, prohibit reasonable agreements between them as to the rates at which merchandise shall be carried. And mark the contrast of what is prohibited. In one case the restraint, it may be, of a whim—certainly of nothing that affects the ability of an employee to perform his duties; nothing, therefore, which is of any material interest to the carrier; in the other case a restraint of a carefully considered policy which had as its motive great material interests and benefits to the railroads, and, in the opinion of many, to the public. May such action be restricted, must it give way to the public welfare, while the other, moved, it may be, by prejudice and antagonism, is intrenched impregnably in the Fifth Amendment of the Constitution against regulation in the public interest." Justice McKenna, dissenting, Adair *v.* United States, 208 U. S., 189.

Possibly another justice came nearer the truth in the matter as popularly understood when he said: "I confess that I think the right to make contracts at will that has been derived from the word liberty in the amendments has been stretched to its extreme by the decisions." Justice Holmes, dissenting, *ibid.*, 208 U. S., 191.

[1] *Supra*, p. 103. [2] *Supra*, p. 110.

The Justices *v.* Murray,[1] though decided on a provision in the constitutional Bill of Rights, really has a political aspect, as the most important question involved was not that of protection to an individual, but that of hampering the administration of the national government in hostile states or sections by interfering with its officers. The statute involved in this case provided that an action against a United States officer in a state court might be taken to a federal tribunal and opened anew after the rendition of judgment in the trial court. Since, however, according to the decision in Tennessee *v.* Davis,[2] Congress has the power to provide that cases of this character may be removed from a state to a federal court before judgment is rendered, the point involved in The Justices *v.* Murray is not as vital as might appear; if for any reason injustice is feared in the trial of a national officer before the state tribunals, this injustice may be avoided by removing the case at once to the federal courts.

Other of the cases included in this section, Boyd *v.* United States[3] and Kirby *v.* United States,[4] are concerned only with a particular class of individuals, and interest the public at large but little. The case of Counselman *v.* Hitchcock,[5] however, has a present and general interest, but by making the immunity somewhat wider Congress was able to accomplish the purpose intended by the act nullified in this case.

In the Monongahela Navigation Co. *v.* United States[6] the court emphasized individual property rights and lost sight of the interests which the community may have

[1] *Supra*, p. 104. [2] 100 U. S., 257. [3] *Supra*, p. 105.

[4] *Supra*, p. 110. [5] *Supra*, p. 107.

[6] *Supra*, p. 108.

had in the question at issue. Since, however, the decision was conclusive only on one point, namely, that the value of the franchise belonging to the company must be considered in case the government took possession of the property, and as it did not indicate either the value of that franchise or any specific method of determining the value, but left both open questions to be decided by the court below, private franchise rights were not necessarily so strongly intrenched by this case as to preclude entirely the interests of the community. But in the most recent instance in which a federal statute was nullified because of conflict with the constitutional Bill of Rights, Adair *v*. United States,[1] the court while ostensibly upholding these individual privileges, made a decision which is probably diametrically opposed to the spirit of the freedom supposed to be guaranteed by the first ten amendments, and the supporting argument is based on an ancient theory of individual rights rather than upon any consideration of actual conditions.

The court, because of its power to nullify a federal statute in conflict with the civil rights clauses of the constitution, has prevented Congress in two instances[2] from going to extremes in hostile class legislation and it will probably now be commended for both of these opinions. Whether it was commended for the *ex parte* Garland decision forty-five years ago when it was rendered is, of course, quite a different question. At least four[3] of the decisions in this section are of general and present importance and others are of present but minor value. On the whole, then, it is probably safe to say

[1] *Supra*, p. 111.

[2] *Ex parte* Garland and Wong Wing *v*. United States.

[3] The Justices *v*. Murray; Counselman *v*. Hitchcock; Monongahela Navigation Co. *v*. United States; Adair *v*. United States.

that the court has made no great use of its power to nullify statutes in this particular class of cases and, excepting Adair *v.* United States, while subjecting itself to no great amount of adverse criticism, can be commended for most of its decisions. In the Adair case, however, the court has probably, wittingly or unwittingly, failed really to protect private rights and liberty.

Section IV.—Ultra vires acts of Congress not included in the above three classifications:

19 How.,	393,	Scott *v.* Sandford, 1856.
8 Wall.,	603,	Hepburn *v.* Griswold, 1869.
157 U. S.,	429,	Pollock *v.* Farmers Loan & Trust Co., 1894.
158 U. S.,	601,	Pollock *v.* Farmers Loan & Trust Co., 1894.
181 U. S.,	283,	Fairbank *v.* United States, 1903.
197 U. S.,	516,	Rassmussen *v.* United States, 1905.

After the court had, in Marbury *v.* Madison, 1803, successfully defended its own jurisdiction and independence and vindicated its claimed power to annul an act of Congress, if it deemed there was a conflict between such act and the constitution, it did not again exercise this power for over half a century. The court's next use of this right after the above-mentioned case was Scott *v.* Sandford,[1] in 1856, when it attempted to settle a fundamental political and social problem which up to that time had baffled the best efforts of both the executive and legislative departments, as well as the thought and efforts of statesmen and reformers outside of these departments. The decision has been judicially described as follows:

[1] 19 How., 393.

It was said of the case of Dred Scott *v.* Sanford, that this court, there overruled the action of two generations, virtually inserted a new clause in the Constitution, changed its character, and made a new departure in the workings of the federal government.[1]

The question thus attempted to be settled was soon afterward really solved by the more drastic method of the sword and consequently the decision had little or no practical legal force. It did succeed, however, in drawing down upon the court grave and severe censure, and illustrates, at least in one great crisis of our national life, how inadequate the court was, how little comprehension it had of the limits of its own powers or of the real importance of the question it thus attempted to solve and its small knowledge of the temper of the public.

Shortly after the close of the Civil War the court was again called upon to pass judgment on what had become an important political question. Laboring under the financial difficulties of the War, Congress had authorized the issue of treasury notes and enacted that the notes should be legal tender for all debts with certain named exceptions. In Hepburn *v.* Griswold[2] the question presented was whether Congress had power to make such notes a legal tender for debts which, when contracted, were payable in gold and silver. The court, in a long opinion, decided that Congress did not have this authority principally because it was not an appropriate and plainly adapted means for carrying out any of the enumerated powers of that body; because it was contrary to the spirit of the constitution inasmuch as it was a law impairing the obligation of contracts; and finally

[1] Justice Harlan dissenting, Civil Rights Cases, 109 U. S., 57.

[2] 8 Wall., 603.

because it was contrary to the due process clause of the fifth amendment. This is the first time that this clause had been mentioned as a basis for declaring a federal act unconstitutional and was not elaborated to any great extent.[1]

In Pollock *v.* Farmers Loan and Trust Company[2] the court again gave judgment on the financial powers of Congress and again limited federal activities in this line. In this case the court, while not prohibiting a tax on all

[1] In this case the court again took the wrong side of a political question. The decision was popularly opposed and both Congress and the public hesitated to accept it as a final determination of the question, the prestige of the court failing to give its conclusions the moral finality which is necessary if its rulings are to be accepted without protest by the public. The determination of the court in this case was, by conference among the justices, made in November, 1869, and the opinion given out in February, 1870. At the time of the conference there were eight justices on the bench and Justice Grier, after some wavering, had agreed that the Legal Tender act was but partially valid, but before the opinion was made public, this Justice, now aged and infirm, at the request of his colleagues on the bench, had resigned. Hence the decision was really a decision by five, three dissenting, though when the opinion was actually read, but four of the concurring justices were on the bench. (See Rhodes, *History of the United States*, vol. vi, p. 258 *et seq.;* also Justice Joseph P. Bradley, *Miscellaneous Writings*, p. 73.) The two vacancies after Justice Grier's resignation were filled in such a way that the minority of three became a majority of five. In May, 1871, in the Legal Tender Cases, 11 Wall., 682, Hepburn *v.* Griswold was largely overturned, although opinions in the case did not appear until January, 1872 (12 Wall., 457). In this case, as in the Dred Scott case, a means was found of changing an unpopular decision of the Supreme Court on a political question—in this instance by a change in the personnel of the court.

In Juillard v. Greenman, 110 U. S., 421, a still more sweeping decision was rendered on this point. In the Legal Tender Cases the power of Congress was upheld largely as a war power, but in Juillard v. Greenman the same authority was conceded to vest in Congress, though in a time of entire peace, thus completely overturning anything that may have been left of the decision in Hepburn v. Griswold.

[2] 157 U. S., 429, and a rehearing, 158 U. S., 601.

incomes, did make it impossible to levy a tax on large classes of them and caused a federal tax of this nature to be economically undesirable. This decision was made, too, in face of the fact that the direct taxes which Congress could only levy by apportionment had been confined to narrow limits in various cases;[1] that the United States had had an income tax for several years during and immediately following the Civil War; and also in face of the fact that the court in passing upon a similar statute in 1880[2] upheld it and declared "that direct taxes, within the meaning of the constitution, are only capitation taxes, as expressed in that instrument, and taxes on real estate." In the two hearings of Pollock *v.* Farmers Loan and Trust Company, the court refused specifically to overturn the findings of the Springer case but at all events, under this decision, a federal income tax is practically impossible.[3]

[1] See *e. g.*, Hylton *v.* United States, 3 Dall., 171; Pacific Insurance Co. *v.* Soule, 7 Wall., 433; Scholey *v.* Rew, 23 Wall., 331; Veazie Bank *v.* Fenno, 8 Wall., 533.

[2] Springer *v.* United States, 102 U. S., 586.

[3] Justice Field, in a separate concurring opinion, less discreet than the other justices, says: "Here I close my opinion. I could not say less in view of questions of such gravity that go down to the very foundation of the government. If the provisions of the Constitution can be set aside by an act of Congress, where is the course of usurpation to end? The present assault upon capital is but the beginning. It will be but the stepping-stone to others, larger and more sweeping, till our political contests will become a war of the poor against the rich; a war constantly growing in intensity and bitterness.

'If the court sanctions the power of discriminating taxation, and nullifies the uniformity mandate of the Constitution,' as said by one who has been all his life a student of our institutions, 'it will mark the hour when the sure decadence of our present government will commence.' If the purely arbitrary limitation of $4000 in the present law can be sustained, none having less than that amount of income being assessed or taxed for the support of the government, the limitations of

In order to obtain funds for the war with Spain, in an internal revenue act of June, 1898,[1] Congress provided among other things that, in effect, bills of lading for export merchandise should pay a stamp tax of eleven cents. The court held[2] that a tax on a bill of lading was equivalent to a tax on the goods themselves, and hence in conflict with the constitutional prohibition of taxes on exported articles.[3] This is a case of no great importance so far as the point decided is concerned, and while it limited the financial powers of Congress it did this but slightly.

The court passed on a political question in Rassmussen *v.* United States.[4] The principal question at issue in this case was whether the constitution applied to Alaska and limited Congress in its general legislative power over the territory. As previously mentioned, the court held the constitution did apply. While the question has a political aspect, the ruling can affect only those parts of the United States over which Congress has general legislative control, and does not necessarily apply to all those. This limits the decision territorially to so great an extent as to deprive it of any general importance.

future Congresses may be fixed at a much larger sum, at five or ten or twenty thousand dollars, parties possessing an income of that amount alone being bound to bear the burdens of government; or the limitation may be designated at such an amount as a board of 'walking delegates' may deem necessary." 157 U. S., 607.

[1] 30 Statutes at Large, 448.

[2] Fairbank *v.* United States, 181 U. S., 283.

[3] Article 1, section 9.

[4] 197 U. S., 516. See also *supra*, note, p. 111.

SUMMARY

In the preceding portions of this chapter an attempt has been made to analyze the character of the federal statutes annulled, and to indicate as far as possible the reasons for such nullifications. In closing, an attempt will be made to summarize regarding the activities of the Supreme Court in declaring federal statutes unconstitutional, and point out how much of a factor in our national life the court has been because of this power.

Although the inviolability of the constitutional powers of the three great branches of the government is supposed to be one of the most fundamental principles of the constitution and one which would be most solicitously protected by the court, we have seen that comparatively few statutes have been annulled because of their conflict with this principle. In all such cases, too, with but one exception, the court was only protecting its own jurisdiction. It cannot be said, therefore, that because of this constitutional doctrine the court has improperly extended its powers nor taken any great part in our national life, and hence subjects itself to neither friendly nor hostile criticism.[1]

Under the second class, the disturbance of federal relations and encroachments on the powers of the states, the court by its interpretation of the fourteenth amendment has very greatly increased its own power and jurisdiction and made the federal judiciary a larger factor in our

[1] This statement applies to the issues decided. The decision in Marbury *v.* Madison did, of course, make the Supreme Court a large potential factor in national life, but the doctrine therein asserted could as well have been attached to any other constitutional case that came up. It so happened that a statute held to interfere with the constitutional position of the judiciary offered the first convenient vehicle for the promulgation of the doctrine.

government than ever before. This is particularly true, since the decisions affecting the more recent industrial and social legislation, from the nature of things, can have no exact precedent, and the court, bound by no more definite a constitutional principle than due process of law, has very wide discretion in determining what state legislation shall be considered valid and what shall not. As the final authority in many instances on constitutional questions, the Supreme Court of the United States is in a position to negative whatever it considers objectionable in the case of state statutes of this nature and in a general way to guide and influence this social and industrial legislation. Also Congress in its attempts to deal with some of these newer problems was partially checked by the court. It is also worthy of note that all of the decisions classified under this section which have been most severely criticised, have been rendered since 1883 and two of them since 1907. The decisions prior to 1883 are probably not open to any severe criticism so far as the actual points at issue are concerned.

In regard to the civil rights guaranteed by the constitution to the individual, the court has been a rather efficient but not an aggressive protector of such rights and it can probably be commended for the numerical majority of its decisions along this line. On the other hand there is grave doubt as to the soundness of the doctrines laid down in Adair *v.* United States and possibly also those asserted in Monongahela Navigation Co. *v.* United States.

In regard to questions involving any important political policy it can probably be as safely said that the court has uniformly and signally failed whenever it attempted to settle such a question by nullifying a federal statute. In some minor cases as Rassmussen *v.*

United States,[1] and Fairbank *v.* United States[2] the court did finally settle a question of this nature but, as already explained, these were of but narrow application and did not excite the interest of, nor effect, the public at large.

The first case of this sort was Scott *v.* Sandford[3] when the court, in the opinion of some, unnecessarily overturned a statute which had been enacted with the expectation of settling what was perhaps the greatest question which has ever confronted this country. As previously mentioned, the decision, so far as a large part of the public was concerned, only brought down censure on the court and gave the problem no more the appearance of a settled question than it had before this judicial determination was made. Likewise in Hepburn *v.* Griswold,[4] the decision according to popular belief was wrong and because of certain changes occurring within the court the ruling was overturned in a short time after it was made. The public again refused to accept the court's determination.

No one at the present time probably will contend that the finding in the Pollock case settled the income-tax question so far as public sentiment is concerned. There has been constantly popular argument to the effect that this decision was not correct and considerable agitation to have Congress re-enact such a tax and at least allow the court the opportunity to pass again on the question.[5] The decision has, however, led to the use of our constitutional machinery in a successful attempt to secure an amendment as the most feasible way to settle the ques-

[1] *Supra*, p. 121.

[2] *Supra*, p. 121.

[3] *Supra*, p. 117.

[4] *Supra*, p. 118.

[5] See *e. g.*, *Congressional Record*, vol. xliv, pt. 4, p. 4408; *ibid.*, vol. xliv, Appendix, p. 119; *ibid.*, vol. xxxi, pt. 8, pp. 358 and 381.

tion and obtain what the judicial branch of the government prohibited. Thus in those instances in which the court, dealing with problems now solved, attempted, by nullifying federal statute, to settle questions of real and vital interest to a large part of the public it has failed.

In three of the more recent cases in which federal statutes have been annulled, Employers Liability Cases,[1] Adair *v.* United States,[2] and Keller *v.* United States,[3] the court reviewed some of the social and industrial problems which are so hedged around by constitutional difficulties as to make most attempted solutions of doubtful validity. In the Employers Liability Cases a compromise decision was rendered which leaves the United States government considerable freedom in some directions though curtailing it in others. In Keller *v.* United States the court absolutely prohibited to the United States the use of one of the effective means of dealing with a great social evil, though fairness compels the statement that the decision was probably in harmony with previous opinions regarding the relative powers of the United States and the states. In Adair *v.* United States the court made a decision based on the individualistic theories of a century ago. Moreover, in this case the due process clause was first seriously applied. If we may judge from the decisions based on the due process clause in the fourteenth amendment and applying to the states, the court has it in its power to make the similar clause in the fifth amendment cover practically all federal legislation dealing with new problems concerning which there are few or no precedents. If the court does make this entirely possible extension of its power, then the legislation dealing with the more recent and pressing questions is under the control of the popularly inaccessible justices of the

[1] *Supra*, p. 95. [2] *Supra*, p. 111. [3] *Supra*, p. 97.

Supreme Court. We have already seen that in at least one of the greatest crises of the country the Supreme Court failed, and instead of a final solution of a great problem by judicial procedure, that high tribunal's decisions resulted only in increased confusion. It is believed by many that the United States is now facing another real crisis because of the unsatisfactory character of present social and industrial conditions. In the light of a knowledge of the achievements of the Supreme Court in the past, is the nation justified in believing that that tribunal will wisely exercise this large control over national legislation affecting present vital problems which it may, and possibly will, exercise because of its power, readily used in recent times, to nullify statutes under elastic clauses of the constitution?

It is quite true of course that Hamilton, Franklin, Madison and the others who participated in the framing of the constitution did not think that any thing in that document would give to the federal government power to pursue the "white slave" traffic to its domicile in the states; nor permit the national government to regulate the relations between master and servant when these were engaged in interstate commerce and to protect the employee from certain oppressions of his employer. It is equally true that the same framers of the constitution had no thought that they had given the national government control over telegraphs,[1] or over the interstate transmission of lottery tickets,[2] yet the Supreme Court has found these powers impliedly given to the national government by the constitution. Again, although

[1] See *e. g.*, Pensacola Telegraph Co. *v.* Western Union Telegraph Co., 96 U. S., 1; Telegraph Co. *v.* Texas, 105 U. S., 460.

[2] Champion *v.* Ames, 188 U. S., 321.

originally the court followed the common law rule of England that admiralty jurisdiction extends only to tide waters, when that rule was found insufficient because of the vast extent of inland water in this country, the court extended its authority and accepted admiralty jurisdiction over the fresh-water rivers of the country.[1] In this instance the court, without any additional legislative authority, simply extended its jurisdiction by its own decisions to meet the exigencies of new circumstances which the old rule did not fit. May it not be reasonably expected and demanded of the court that it allow as great a legislative discretion and show as great an eagerness and ability to meet the exigencies of changed circumstances in cases involving human and social rights as it has to meet those involving commerce and property rights?

If the Supreme Court is not voluntarily sufficiently liberal and tolerant and does not allow sufficient legislative discretion in dealing with present day problems, what remedy is there? There are at least two possible solutions. One would be to amend the constitution either by giving the national government specific powers to deal with certain questions or by limiting the power of the court itself. The other method is by proper attention to the personnel of the court and by popular criticism of its decisions to influence its attitude towards certain questions. The constitution is amended with the greatest difficulty but it is doubtful if the other method offers any easier or more feasible remedy when existing conditions are considered.

[1] *Cf.* The Thomas Jefferson, 10 Wheaton, 428, and The Hine *v.* Trevor, 4 Wall., 555.

APPENDIX I

Table of Cases in which National Legislation has been Declared Contrary to the National Constitution by the Supreme Court of the United States.[1]

Number of Opinions.			Number of Dissenting Justices.
	13 How. 52. United States *v.* Todd	1794	..
1	1 Cranch 137. Marbury *v.* Madison	1803	..
9	19 How. 393. Scott *v.* Sanford	1856	2
1	2 Wall. 561; 117 U. S. 697. Gordon *v.* United States.	1864	..
2	4 Wall. 333. *Ex parte* Garland	1866	4
1	6 Wall. 160. Reichart *v.* Felps	1867	..
1	7 Wall. 571. The Alicia	1868	..
2	8 Wall. 603. Hepburn *v.* Griswold	1869	3
1	9 Wall. 41. United States *v.* DeWitt	1869	..
1	9 Wall. 274. The Justices *v.* Murray	1869	..
2	11 Wall. 113. The Collector *v.* Day	1870	1
2	13 Wall. 128. United States *v.* Klein.	1871	2
3	17 Wall. 322. United States *v.* Railroad Co.	1873	3
3	92 U. S. 214. United States *v.* Reese	1875	2
1	95 U. S. 670. United States *v.* Fox	1877	..
1	100 U. S. 82. Trade Mark Cases	1879	..
1	106 U. S. 629. United States *v.* Harris	1882	..[2]
2	109 U. S. 3. Civil Rights Cases	1883	1
2	116 U. S. 616. Boyd *v.* United States	1885	..
1	127 U. S. 540. Callan *v.* Wilson	1887	..
1	142 U. S. 547. Counselman *v.* Hitchcock	1891	1
1	148 U. S. 312. Navigation Co. *v.* United States	1894	..
3	157 U. S. 429. Pollock *v.* Farmers Loan Company	1894	2

[1] All cases in the appendices are dated according to the term of court in which they were decided, *e. g.*, cases listed under 1911 include all cases decided at the term convening in that year although the court did not adjourn until May, 1912.

[2] In Baldwin *v.* Franks, 120 U S. 678, the validity of the same statute considered in United States *v.* Harris, was questioned and the court reaffirmed its previous decision.

5	158 U. S. 601.	Pollock *v.* Farmers Loan Company...	1894	4
2	163 U. S. 228.	Wong Wing *v.* United States	1895	..
1	174 U. S. 47.	Kirby *v.* United States	1899	2
2	181 U. S. 283.	Fairbank *v.* United States	1901	3
1	190 U. S. 127.	James *v.* Bowman	1903	2
3	197 U. S. 516.	Rassmussen *v.* United States	1905	..
5	207 U. S. 463.	Employers Liability Cases	1907	4
3	208 U. S. 161.	Adair *v.* United States	1907	2
2	213 U. S. 138.	Keller *v.* United States	1908	3
1	213 U. S. 297.	United States *v.* Evans	1908	..
1	219 U. S. 346.	Muskrat *v.* United States	1910	..

APPENDIX II

Table of Cases in which State Constitutions, State and Territorial Statutes and Municipal Ordinances have been Declared Contrary to the National Constitution by the Supreme Court of the United States.[1]

Number of Opinions.				Number of Dissenting Justices.
1	5 Cranch 115. United States *v.* Peters	Pa.	1809	..
2	6 Cranch 87. Fletcher *v.* Peck	Ga.	1810	1[2]
1	7 Cranch 164. New Jersey *v.* Wilson	N. J.	1812	..
1	9 Cranch 43. Terrett *v.* Taylor	Va.	1815	..
1	4 Wheaton 122. Sturges *v.* Crowninshield	N. Y.	1819	..
1[3]	4 Wheaton 209. McMillan *v.* McNeill	La.	1819	..
1	4 Wheaton 316. McCulloch *v.* Maryland	Md.	1819	..
3	4 Wheaton 518. Dartmouth College *v.* Woodward	N. H.	1819	1
1	6 Wheaton 131. Farmers & Mechanics Bank *v.* Smith	Pa.	1821	..
2	8 Wheaton 1. Green *v.* Biddle	Ky.	1823	..
1	8 Wheaton 464. Society, etc. *v.* New Haven	Vt.	1823	..
2	9 Wheaton 1. Gibbons *v.* Ogden	N. Y.	1824	..
2	9 Wheaton 738. Osborn *v.* U. S. Bank	Ohio.	1824	1
[4]	12 Wheaton 213. Ogden *v.* Saunders	N. Y.	1827	3
2	12 Wheaton 419. Brown *v.* Maryland	Md.	1827	1
3a	2 Peters 449. Weston *v.* City of Charleston	S. C.	1829	2
4	4 Peters 410. Craig *v.* Missouri	Mo.	1830	3

[1] This list includes only cases in which legislative enactments were passed and declared void after the adoption of the U. S. constitution.

[2] Partly concurring, partly dissenting.

[3] The constitutional ruling in this case was later affirmed in a Maryland case, Cook *v.* Moffat, 5 How. 295.

[4] Different points in this case were argued at different times. At first hearing five opinions written, three justices dissenting and part of the statute upheld; at second hearing one opinion written, three justices dissenting, and the statute partially nullified.

2	6 Peters 515.	Worcester *v.* Georgia	Ga.	1832	1
1[1]	6 Peters 635.	Boyle *v.* Zacharie	Md.	1832	..
1	16 Peters 435.	Dobbins *v.* Commissioners	Pa.	1842	..
7	16 Peters 539.	Prigg *v.* Pennsylvania	Pa.	1842	1
2	1 Howard 311.	Bronson *v.* Kinzie	Ill.	1843	1
2	2 Howard 608.	McCracken *v.* Hayward	Ill.	1844	..
1	3 Howard 133.	Gordon *v.* The Tax Court	Md.	1845	..
3[2]	3 Howard 151	Searight *v.* Stokes	Pa.	1845	2
2[3]	3 Howard 720.	Neil *v.* Ohio	Ohio	1845	1
3	6 Howard 301.	Planters' Bank *v.* Sharp	Miss.	1848	2
8	7 Howard 283.	Passenger Cases	N. Y. and Mass.	1849	4
2	10 Howard 190.	Woodruff *v.* Trapnall	Ark.	1850	4
1e	11 Howard 437.	Webster *v.* Reid	Iowa	1850	..
1[4]	12 Howard 293.	Achison *v.* Huddleson	Md.	1851	..
2	14 Howard 268.	Vincennes University *v.* Indiana	Ind.	1852	3
3	15 Howard 304.	Curran *v.* Arkansas	Ark.	1853	3
5[5]	16 Howard 369.	State Bank *v.* Knoop	Ohio	1853	3
3	17 Howard 596.	Hays *v.* Pacific Mail Co.	Cal.	1854	1
2	18 Howard 331.	Dodge *v.* Woolsey	Ohio	1855	3
2e	20 Howard 558.	Irvine *v.* Marshall	Minn.	1857	4
1[6]h	22 Howard 227.	Sinnot *v.* Davenport	Ala.	1859	..
1	24 Howard 169.	Almy *v.* California	Cal.	1860	..
1	24 Howard 461.	Howard *v.* Bugbee	Ala.	1860	..
1	2 Black 620.	Bank of Commerce *v.* New York.	N. Y.	1862	..
1	2 Wall. 10.	Hawthorne *v.* Calef	Me.	1864	..

[1] The constitutional ruling in this case was reaffirmed in Cook *v.* Moffatt, 5 Howard 295.

[2] Statute partly annulled because in conflict with contract between Pennsylvania and United States.

[3] Statute partly annulled because in conflict with contract between Ohio and United States.

[4] Statute partly annulled because in conflict with contract between Maryland and United States.

[5] The constitutional ruling made in this case and under different circumstances in Dodge *v.* Woolsey, 18 How. 331, was reaffirmed in Bank *v.* Debolt, 18 How. 380; Jefferson Bank *v.* Skelly, 1 Black 436; Franklin Bank *v.* Ohio, 1 Black 474; Wright *v.* Sill, 2 Black 544, all being cases based on Ohio statutes.

[6] The statute involved in this case was again held invalid in Foster *v.* Davenport, 22 How. 244.

1[1]	2 Wall. 200.	Bank Tax Case	N. Y.	1864	..
2	3 Wall. 51.	The Binghamton Bridge	N. Y.	1865	3
2h	3 Wall. 573.	Van Allen *v.* The Assessors	N. Y.	1865	..
1	4 Wall. 143.	McGee *v.* Mathis	Ark.	1866	..
2b	4 Wall. 277.	Cummings *v.* Missouri	Mo.	1866	4
1h	4 Wall. 411.	The Moses Taylor	Cal.	1866	..
1	4 Wall. 459.	Bradley *v.* The People	Ill.	1866	..
1	4 Wall. 535.	Von Hoffman *v.* City of Quincy	Ill.	1866	..
1h	4 Wall. 555.	The Hine *v.* Trevor	Iowa	1866	..
1	5 Wall. 290.	Christmas *v.* Russell	Miss.	1866	..
1	5 Wall. 737.	The Kansas Indians	Kans.	1866	..
1	5 Wall. 761.	The New York Indians	N. Y.	1866	..
1	6 Wall. 31.	Steamship Co. *v.* Port Wardens	La.	1867	..
2	6 Wall. 35.	Crandall *v.* Nevada	Nev.	1867	..
1h	7 Wall. 26.	Bank *v.* The Supervisors	N. Y.	1868	..
2	7 Wall. 262.	Railroad Co. *v.* Jackson	Pa.	1868	2
1	7 Wall. 624.	The Belfast	Ala.	1868	..
1	8 Wall. 44.	Furman *v.* Nichol	Tenn.	1868	..
2	8 Wall. 430.	Home of the Friendless *v.* Rouse	Mo.	1869	3
2	8 Wall. 439.	Washington University *v.* Rouse	Mo.	1869	3
1e	11 Wall. 610.	Dunphy *v.* Kleinsmith	Mont.	1870	..
1	12 Wall. 204.	State Tonnage Tax Cases	Ala.	1870	..
2	12 Wall. 418.	Ward *v.* Maryland	Md.	1870	..
1	13 Wall. 92.	Gibson *v.* Chouteau	Mo.	1871	2
1	13 Wall. 264.	Wilmington Ry. *v.* Reid	N. C.	1871	..
2b	13 Wall. 646.	White *v.* Hart	Ga.	1871	1
2b	13 Wall. 654.	Osborn *v.* Nicholson	Ark.	1871	1
1b	14 Wall. 661.	Delmas *v.* Insurance Co.	La.	1871	..
2	15 Wall. 232.	State Freight Tax Case	Pa.	1872	2
2	15 Wall. 300.	State Tax on Foreign-Held Bonds	Pa.	1872	4
1d	15 Wall. 610.	Gunn *v.* Barry	Ga.	1872	..
2	16 Wall. 234.	Pierce *v.* Carskadon	W. Va.	1872	1
1	16 Wall. 244.	Humphrey *v.* Pegues	Ga.	1872	..
1	16 Wall. 314.	Walker *v.* Whitehead	Ga.	1872	..
2	19 Wall. 1.	Barings *v.* Dabney	S. C.	1873	..
1[2]	19 Wall. 581.	Peete *v.* Morgan	Tex.	1873	..
3	20 Wall. 36.	Pacific Railway Co. *v.* McGuire	Mo.	1873	2
2	20 Wall. 445.	Insurance Co. *v.* Morse	Wis.	1874	2
1a	20 Wall. 577.	Cannon *v.* New Orleans	La.	1874	..

[1] The constitutional point in this case was further elaborated in The Banks *v.* The Mayor, 7 Wall. 16.

[2] An ordinance adopted by a constitutional convention held invalid.

2	20 Wall. 655.	Loan Association *v.* Topeka	Kans.	1874	1
2	91 U. S. 3.	Wilmington & Weldon R. R. *v.* King	N. C.	1875	1
1	91 U. S. 275.	Welton *v.* Missouri	Mo.	1875	..
1	92 U. S. 259.	Henderson *v.* New York	N. Y.	1875	..
1	92 U. S. 275.	Chy Lung *v.* Freeman	Cal.	1875	..
1	94 U. S. 238.	Inman Steamship Co. *v.* Tinker	N. Y.	1876	..
1	94 U. S. 246.	Foster *v.* Master of New Orleans	La.	1876	..
1	154 U. S. 626.	Morrill *v.* Wisconsin	Wis.	1876	..
1	95 U. S. 104.	New Jersey *v.* Yard	N. J.	1877	..
1	95 U. S. 465.	Railroad Co. *v.* Husen	Mo.	1877	..
2	95 U. S. 485.	Hall *v.* DeCuir	La.	1877	..
2	95 U. S. 679.	Farrington *v.* Tennessee	Tenn.	1877	3
3	96 U. S. 1.	Pensacola Telegraph Co. *v.* Western Union Telegraph Co.	Fla.	1877	2
2a	96 U. S. 432.	Murray *v.* Charleston	S. C.	1877	2
3d	96 U. S. 595.	Edwards *v.* Kearzey	N. C.	1877	1
4	97 U. S. 454.	Keith *v.* Clark	Tenn.	1878	3
1	97 U. S. 566.	Cook *v.* Pennsylvania	Pa.	1878	..
1	99 U. S. 309.	University *v.* People	Ill.	1878	..
2	100 U. S. 303.	Strauder *v.* West Virginia	W. Va.	1879	2
2c	100 U. S. 434.	Guy *v.* Baltimore	Md.	1879	1
1	102 U. S. 123.	Tiernan *v.* Rinker	Tex.	1880	..
2	102 U. S. 672.	Hartman *v.* Greenhow	Va.	1880	1
1	103 U. S. 5.	Hall *v.* Wisconsin	Wis.	1880	..
1	103 U. S. 344.	Webber *v.* Virginia	Va.	1880	..
2	103 U. S. 358.	Wolff *v.* New Orleans	La.	1880	..
1	105 U. S. 278.	Louisiana *v.* Pilsbury	La.	1881	..
2d	105 U. S. 362.	Asylum *v.* New Orleans	La.	1881	2
1	105 U. S. 460.	Telegraph Co. *v.* Texas	Tex.	1881	..
1[1]	105 U. S. 733.	Ralls County Court *v.* U. S.	Mo.	1881	..
1	106 U. S. 487.	Parkersburg *v.* Brown	W. Va.	1882	..
1	107 U. S. 59.	People *v.* Compagnie Transatlantique	N. Y.	1882	..
2b	107 U. S. 221.	Kring *v.* Missouri	Mo.	1882	4
1	111 U. S. 716.	Nelson *v.* St. Martin's Parish	La.	1883	..
1a	112 U. S. 69.	Moran *v.* New Orleans	La.	1884	..
1c	113 U. S. 1.	Cole *v.* LaGrange	Mo.	1884	..
1	114 U. S. 196.	Gloucester Ferry Co. *v.* Pa.	Pa.	1884	..
2	114 U. S. 270.	Virginia Coupon Cases	Va.	1884	4
1	115 U. S. 566.	Effinger *v.* Kenney	Va.	1885	..

[1] The constitutional ruling in this case was reaffirmed in Scotland County Court *v.* Hill, 140 U. S. 41.

1d	115 U. S. 650.	New Orleans Gas Co. *v.* La. Light Co.	La.	1885	..
1[1]g	115 U. S. 674.	New Orleans Water Co. *v.* Rivers	La.	1885	..
1	115 U. S. 683.	Louisville Gas Co. *v.* Citizens Gas Co.	Ky.	1885	..
1	116 U. S. 131.	Fisk *v.* Jefferson Police Jury	La.	1885	..
1	116 U. S. 289.	Mobile *v.* Watson	Ala.	1885	..
1	116 U. S. 446.	Walling *v.* Michigan	Mich.	1885	..
1	116 U. S. 572.	Royall *v.* Virginia	Va.	1885	..
1[2]	117 U. S. 34.	Pickard *v.* Pullman Southern Car Company	Tenn.	1885	..
1	117 U. S. 151.	Van Brocklin *v.* Tennessee	Tenn.	1885	..
1h	118 U. S. 90.	Spraigue *v.* Thompson	Ga.	1885	..
1a	118 U. S. 356.	Yick Wo *v.* Hopkins	Cal.	1885	..
2	118 U. S. 557.	Railroad Co. *v.* Illinois	Ill.	1886	3
2	120 U. S. 489.	Robbins *v.* Shelby Taxing District	Tenn.	1886	3
2	120 U. S. 502.	Corson *v.* Maryland	Md.	1886	..
1	121 U. S. 186.	Barron *v.* Burnside	Iowa	1886	..
1	121 U. S. 230.	Fargo *v.* Michigan	Mich.	1886	..
1	122 U. S. 284.	Seibert *v.* Lewis	Mo.	1886	..
1	122 U. S. 326.	Philadelphia S. S. Co. *v.* Pennsylvania	Pa.	1886	..
1	122 U. S. 347.	Western Union Tel. Co. *v.* Pendleton	Ind.	1886	..
3	125 U. S. 465.	Bowman *v.* Chicago & North W. Ry. Co.	Iowa	1887	3
1h	125 U. S. 530.	Western Union Tel. Co. *v.* Mass.	Mass.	1887	..
1d	127 U. S. 1.	California *v.* Pacific Ry. Company	Cal.	1887	..
1	127 U. S. 411.	Ratterman *v.* Western Union Tel. Co.	Ohio	1887	..
1a	127 U. S. 640.	Leloup *v.* Port of Mobile	Ala.	1887	..
1	128 U. S. 129.	Asher *v.* Texas	Tex.	1888	..
2	129 U. S. 141.	Stoutenburgh *v.* Hennick	D. C.	1888	1
1	132 U. S. 472.	Western Union Tel. Co. *v.* Ala.	Ala.	1889	..
2	134 U. S. 160.	*Ex parte* Medley	Col.	1889	2

[1] The constitutional ruling in this case was reaffirmed in Water Works Co. *v.* New Orleans Water Co., 120 U. S. 64.

[2] The constitutional ruling in this case was reaffirmed in Tennessee *v.* Pullman Co., 117 U. S. 51.

3[1]	134 U. S. 418.	Railroad v. Minnesota	Minn.	1889	3
2	135 U. S. 100.	Leisy v. Hardin	Iowa	1889	3
2	135 U. S. 161.	Lyng v. Michigan	Mich.	1889	3
1	135 U. S. 662.	McGahey v. Virginia	Va.	1889	..
1a	136 U. S. 104.	McCall v. California	Cal.	1889	3
1	136 U. S. 114.	Norfolk & Western Ry. Co. v. Pa.	Pa.	1889	3
1	136 U. S. 313.	Minnesota v. Barber	Minn.	1889	..
1	138 U. S. 78.	Brimmer v. Rebman	Va.	1890	..
1	140 U. S. 1.	Pennoyer v. McConnaughy	Ore.	1890	..
1	141 U. S. 47	Crutcher v. Kentucky	Ky.	1890	2
1	141 U. S. 62.	Voight v. Wright	Va.	1890	..
1a	147 U. S. 396.	Harman v. Chicago	Ill.	1892	..
1a	153 U. S. 289.	Brennan v. Titusville	Pa.	1893	..
2	153 U. S. 486.	Mobile & Ohio Ry. Co. v. Tennessee	Tenn.	1893	4
1	153 U. S. 628.	Erie Ry. v. Pennsylvania	Penn.	1893	..
2	154 U. S. 204.	Covington & Cincinnati Bridge Co. v. Kentucky	Ky.	1893	..
1h	158 U. S. 98.	Gulf Colorado & S. F. Ry. Co. v. Hefley	Tex.	1894	..
1	161 U. S. 134.	Bank of Commerce v. Tennessee	Tenn.	1895	1[2]
1	163 U. S. 118.	Barnitz v. Beverly	Kans.	1895	..
1	163 U. S. 142.	Illinois Central Ry. v. Illinois	Ill.	1895	..
1	164 U. S. 403.	Mo. Pac. Ry. Co. v. Nebraska	Nebr.	1896	..
2	165 U. S. 58.	Scott v. Donald	S. C.	1896	1
2	165 U. S. 150.	Railroad v. Ellis	Tex.	1896	3
1	165 U. S. 578.	Allgeyer v. Louisiana	La.	1896	..
1e	166 U. S. 464.	American Publishing Co. v. Fisher	Utah	1896	..
1	169 U. S. 466.	Smyth v. Ames	Nebr.	1897	..
1b	170 U. S. 243.	Houston & Tex. Central Ry. v. Texas	Tex.	1897	..
1b	170 U. S. 343.	Thompson v. Utah	Utah	1897	2
2	171 U. S. 1.	Schollenberger v. Pennsylvania	Pa.	1897	2
1	171 U. S. 30.	Collins v. New Hampshire	N. H.	1897	2
1a	172 U. S. 1.	Walla Walla City v. Walla Walla Water Co.	Wash.	1898	..
2	172 U. S. 239.	Blake v. McClung	Tenn.	1898	2

[1] The statute passed on in this case was again held invalid in Minneapolis Railroad Co. v. Minnesota, 134 U. S. 467.

[2] Partly concurring, partly dissenting.

2a	172 U. S. 269.	Norwood *v.* Baker	Ohio	1898	3
1	173 U. S. 193.	Dewey *v.* Des Moines	Iowa	1898	..
1	173 U. S. 276.	Ohio *v.* Thomas	Ohio	1898	..
1	173 U. S. 684.	Railroad Co. *v.* Smith	Mich.	1898	3
2	177 U. S. 66.	Houston & Texas Central R. R. Co. *v.* Texas	Tex.	1899	..
2	177 U. S. 514.	Cleveland, Cincinnati, Chicago & St. L. Ry. Co. *v.* Illinois	Ill.	1899	..
1a	177 U. S. 558.	Los Angeles *v.* Los Angeles Water Co.	Cal.	1899	..
3	179 U. S. 223.	Stearns *v.* Minnesota	Minn.	1900	..
1	179 U. S. 302.	Duluth & Iron Range R. R. Co. *v.* St. Louis Co.	Minn.	1900	..
2	183 U. S. 79.	Cotting *v.* Stock Yards Co.	Kans.	1901	..
2b	184 U. S. 27.	Louisville & Nashville R. R. Co. *v.* Eubank	Ky.	1901	2
1a	184 U. S. 368.	Detroit *v.* Detroit Citizens St. Ry. Co.	Mich.	1901	..
2	184 U. S. 540.	Connolly *v.* Sewer Pipe Co.	Ill.	1901	1
1	185 U. S. 27.	Stockard *v.* Morgan	Tenn.	1901	..
1a	187 U. S. 622.	Caldwell *v.* North Carolina	N. C.	1902	..
1	188 U. S. 385.	Ferry Co. *v.* Kentucky	Ky.	1902	2
1	189 U. S. 185.	The Roanoke	Wash.	1902	..
2	191 U. S. 17.	The Robert W. Parsons	N. Y.	1903	4
1	191 U. S. 171.	Allen *v.* Pullman Co.	Tenn.	1903	..
2a	192 U. S. 64.	Postal Telegraph Co. *v.* Taylor	Pa.	1903	2
1a	194 U. S. 517.	Cleveland *v.* Cleveland Ry. Co.	Ohio	1903	..
1	195 U. S. 1.	Bradley *v.* Lightcap	Ill.	1903	..
1a	195 U. S. 223.	Dobbins *v.* Los Angeles	Cal.	1904	..
1	196 U. S. 194.	Central Ry. of Ga. *v.* Murphey	Ga.	1904	..
3	198 U. S. 45.	Lochner *v.* New York	N. Y.	1904	4
2	199 U. S. 194.	Union Transit Co. *v.* Kentucky	Ky.	1905	..
1	201 U. S. 321.	Houston & Texas Central Ry. *v.* Mayes	Tex.	1905	3
1a	201 U. S. 529.	Cleveland *v.* Cleveland Electric R. R.	Ohio	1905	..
1	201 U. S. 543.	Powers *v.* Railroad Co.	Mich.	1905	1
2c	202 U. S. 453.	Vicksburg *v.* Waterworks Co.	Miss.	1905	1
1	202 U. S. 543.	McNeill *v.* Southern Ry. Co.	N.C.	1905	..
1a	203 U. S. 507.	Rearick *v.* Pennsylvania	Pa.	1906	..
1	204 U. S. 103.	American Co. *v.* Colorado	Col.	1906	4
1	205 U. S. 503.	Savings Bank *v.* Des Moines	Iowa	1906	3
2	206 U. S. 129.	Express Co. *v.* Kentucky	Ky.	1906	1
1a	206 U. S. 496.	Vicksburg *v.* Vicksburg Water Company	Miss.	1906	..

1	207 U. S. 127.	Railroad Co. *v.* Wright	Ga.	1907	..
1	208 U. S. 113.	Darnell *v.* Memphis	Tenn.	1907	..
2	209 U. S. 123.	*Ex parte* Young	Minn.	1907	1
2	210 U. S. 217.	Railroad Co. *v.* Texas	Tex.	1907	4
1a	210 U. S. 373.	Londoner *v.* Denver	Col.	1907	2
1	212 U. S. 19.	Willcox *v.* Gas Co.	N. Y.	1908	..
2b	212 U. S. 132.	Louisville & Nashville R. R. *v.* Stockyards	Ky.	1908	3
1	212 U. S. 315.	Nielson *v.* Oregon	Ore.	1908	..
1	214 U. S. 218.	Adams Express Co. *v.* Kentucky	Ky	1908	1
1	215 U. S. 170	Hubert *v.* New Orleans	La.	1909	..
1a	215 U. S. 417.	Minneapolis *v.* Minneapolis Ry.	Minn.	1909	..
1	215 U. S. 515.	Flaherty *v.* Hanson	N. D.	1909	3
3[1]	216 U. S. 1.	Telegraph Co. *v.* Kansas	Kans.	1909	4
1	216 U. S. 146.	Ludwig *v.* Telegraph Co.	Ark.	1909	3
1	216 U. S. 400.	Southern R. R. Co. *v.* Greene	Ala	1909	3
1	217 U. S. 91.	Text Book Co. *v.* Pigg	Kans.	1909	2
1	217 U. S. 136.	St. Louis & Southwestern R. R. Co. *v.* Arkansas	Ark.	1909	1
1	217 U. S. 196.	Missouri Pacific R. R. Co. *v.* Nebraska	Nebr.	1909	2
1	218 U. S. 124.	Dozier *v.* Alabama	Ala.	1909	..
1[2]	218 U. S. 135.	Herndon *v.* Railroad Co.	Mo.	1909	..
2	219 U. S. 219.	Bailey *v.* Alabama	Ala.	1910	2
1	221 U. S. 229.	Oklahoma *v.* Kansas Gas Co.	Okla.	1910	3
1eh	222 U. S. 334.	Berryman *v.* Whitmore College	Wash.	1911	..
1h	222 U. S. 370.	Railroad Co. *v.* Washington	Wash.	1911	..
1h	222 U. S. 424.	Southern R. R. Co. *v.* Reid	N. C.	1911	..
1	223 U. S. 70.	Railroad Co. *v.* Cook Co.	Ky.	1911	..
1	223 U. S. 280.	Railroad Co. *v.* O'Connor	Col.	1911	..
1	223 U. S. 298.	Oklahoma *v.* Express Co.	Okla.	1911	..

[1] The constitutional ruling in this case was reaffirmed in Pullman Co. *v.* Kansas, 216 U. S. 56.

[2] Two statutes partially nullified in this case.

a Municipal ordinance. b State constitution. c Statute and city ordinance. d Constitution and statute. e Territorial statute. g State constitution and municipal ordinance. h In conflict with U. S. statute which Congress had constitutional authority to enact.

APPENDIX III

Statistical Summaries

Summary of National Statutes, State Constitutions and Statutes, and Municipal Ordinances which have been held unconstitutional by the Supreme Court of the United States because of conflict with the National Constitution.[1]

	United States	State	Municipal	Total
1790–1800	1	..	..	1
1800–1810	1	2	..	3
1810–1820	..	6	..	6
1820–1830	..	8	1	9
1830–1840	..	2	..	2
1840–1850	..	11[2]	..	11
1850–1860	1	10[3]	..	11
1860–1870	8	25[4]	..	33
1870–1880	5	39[5]	3[5]	47
1880–1890	4	48[6] [7]	5[6]	57
1890–1900	5	26[8]	4	35
1900–1910	8	40[9]	10	58
1910–1911	..	6[10]	..	6
	33	223	23	279[11]

[1] This list includes only acts passed and declared void after the adoption of the constitution.

[2] Includes one statute of the territory of Iowa.

[3] Includes one statute of the territory of Minnesota.

[4] Includes one statute of the territory of Montana.

[5] Includes Guy *v.* Baltimore, 100 U. S., 434, in which both a state statute and a municipal ordinance were held void.

[6] Includes Cole *v.* LaGrange, 113 U. S., 1, in which both a state statute and a municipal ordinance were held void.

[7] One legislative act of the District of Columbia included.

[8] Includes one statute of the territory of Utah.

[9] Includes Vicksburg *v.* Water Works Co., 202 U. S., 453, in which both a state statute and municipal ordinance were held void.

[10] Includes one statute of the territory of Washington.

[11] The difference in this total and the one appearing in the Statistical Summary in Appendix V is not a real discrepancy but is due to the fact, as indicated in the notes, that in Appendix III some cases are counted twice because two separate legislative enactments were held void in each, and in Appendix V a few cases are listed twice because equally in conflict with two constitutional clauses.

Summary of cases in which a conflict between the National Constitution and Statutes, State Constitutions and Municipal Ordinances was alleged to exist, but the legislation upheld by the Supreme Court of the United States.

	United States	State	Municipal	Total
1790–1800........	1	..	..	1
1800–1810........	2	..	..	2
1810–1820........	4	3	..	7
1820–1830........	2	11[1]	..	13
1830–1840........	2	11[2]	..	13
1840–1850........	5	16[3]	1	22
1850–1860........	5	15	1	21
1860–1870........	13	28	2	43
1870–1880........	27	73[4]	9[4]	109
1880–1890........	31	109[5, 6]	12[5]	152
1890–1900........	40	150[7, 8]	21[8]	211
1900–1910........	53	213[9, 10]	25[9]	291
1910–1911........	..	17[11]	2[11]	19
	185	646	73	904

[1] Includes one statute of the territory of Florida.

[2] Includes Poole *v.* Fleiger, 11 Peters, 185, in which statutes of both North Carolina and Tennessee were upheld.

[3] In the License Cases, 5 Howard, 504, statutes of Rhode Island, New Hampshire, and Massachusetts, were upheld.

[4] Includes Transportation Co. *v.* Wheeling, 99 U. S., 273, in which both a state statute and a municipal ordinance were upheld.

[5] Includes four cases in which both a state statute and a municipal ordinance were upheld.

[6] Includes one statute of the territory of Idaho, one of the territory of Oregon, and one act of the District of Columbia.

[7] Includes five territorial statutes.

[8] Includes four cases in which both state statutes and municipal ordinances were upheld.

[9] Includes eight cases in which both state statutes and municipal ordinances were upheld.

[10] Includes one territorial statute.

[11] Includes Cincinnati *v.* Railroad Co., 223 U. S., 390, in which both a state statute and a municipal ordinance were upheld.

Ratio which statutes held void by the Supreme Court of the United States bear to the total number of statutes contested on constitutional grounds, expressed in per cent.

	Federal Statutes			State Statutes			Municipal Ordinances			All Statutes		
	Nullified	Upheld	Per cent. nullified	Nullified	Upheld	Per cent. nullified	Nullified	Upheld	Per cent. nullified	Nullified	Upheld	Per cent. nullified
1790–1800	1	1	50	..	..	..	..	..	..	1	1	50
1800–1810	1	2	33	2	..	..	..	..	..	3	2	60
1810–1820	..	4	..	6	3	67	..	..	..	6	7	46
1820–1830	..	2	..	8	11	42	1	..	..	9	13	41
1830–1840	..	2	..	2	11	15	..	..	..	2	13	13
1840–1850	..	5	..	11	16	41	..	1	..	11	22	33
1850–1860	1	5	17	10	15	40	..	1	..	11	21	34
1860–1870	8	13	38	25	28	47	..	2	..	33	43	43
1870–1880	5	27	16	39	73	35	3	9	25	47	109	30
1880–1890	4	31	11	48	109	31	5	12	29	57	152	27
1890–1900	5	40	11	26	150	15	4	21	16	35	211	14
1900–1910	8	53	13	40	213	16	10	25	29	58	291	17
1910–1911	..	..	..	6	17	26	..	2	..	6	19	24

APPENDIX IV

Cases in which State Constitutions and Statutes, Territorial Statutes and Municipal Ordinances were nullified by the Federal Supreme Court, Classified by States.

Alabama—

h 22 Howard 227.	Sinnot *v.* Davenport	1859
24 Howard 461.	Howard *v.* Bugbee	1860
7 Wall. 624.	The Belfast	1868
12 Wall. 204.	State Tonnage Tax Cases	1870
116 U. S. 289.	Mobile *v.* Watson	1885
a 127 U. S. 640.	Leloup *v.* Port of Mobile	1887
132 U. S. 472.	Western Union Tel. Co. *v.* Alabama	1889
216 U. S. 400.	Southern R. R. Co. *v.* Greene	1909
218 U. S. 124.	Dozier *v.* Alabama	1909
219 U. S. 219.	Bailey *v.* Alabama	1910
	Total	10

Arizona—

Arkansas—

10 Howard 190.	Woodruff *v.* Trapnall	1850
15 Howard 304.	Curran *v.* Arkansas	1853
4 Wall. 143.	McGee *v.* Mathis	1865
b 13 Wall. 654.	Osborn *v.* Nicholson	1871
216 U. S. 146.	Ludwig *v.* Western Union Telegraph	1909
217 U. S. 136.	Railroad Co. *v.* Arkansas	1909
	Total	6

California—

17 Howard 596.	Hays *v.* Pacific Mail S. S. Co.	1853
24 Howard 169.	Almy *v.* California	1860
h 4 Wall. 411.	The Moses Taylor	1866
92 U. S. 275.	Chy Lung *v.* Freeman	1875
a 118 U. S. 356.	Yick Wo *v.* Hopkins	1885
d 127 U. S. 1.	California *v.* Central Pacific Ry. Co.	1887
a 136 U. S. 104.	McCall *v.* California	1889
a 177 U. S. 558.	Los Angeles *v.* Los Angeles Water Co.	1899
a 195 U. S. 223.	Dobbins *v.* Los Angeles	1904
	Total	9

Colorado—

134 U. S. 160. *Ex parte* Medley 1889
204 U. S. 103. American Co. *v.* Colorado 1906
a 210 U. S. 373. Londoner *v.* Denver 1907
223 U. S. 280. Railroad Co. *v.* O'Connor 1911
Total 4

Connecticut—

Delaware—

Florida—

96 U. S. 1. Pensacola Tel. Co. *v.* Western Union Tel. Co. .. 1877
Total 1

Georgia—

6 Cranch 87. Fletcher *v.* Peck 1810
6 Peters 515. Worcester *v.* Georgia 1832
b 13 Wall. 646. White *v.* Hart 1871
d 15 Wall. 610. Gunn *v.* Barry 1872
16 Wall. 244. Humphrey *v.* Pegues 1872
16 Wall. 314. Walker *v.* Whitehead 1872
h 118 U. S. 90. Spraigue *v.* Thompson 1885
196 U. S. 194. Central Ry. of Ga. *v.* Murphey 1904
207 U. S. 127. Railroad Co. *v.* Wright 1907
Total 9

Idaho—

Illinois—

1 Howard 311. Bronson *v.* Kinzie 1843
2 Howard 608. McCracken *v.* Hayward 1844
h 4 Wall. 459. Bradley *v.* The People 1866
4 Wall. 535. Von Hoffman *v.* City of Quincy 1866
99 U. S. 309. University *v.* The People 1878
118 U. S. 557. W. St. L. & Pacific Ry. Co. *v.* Illinois 1886
a 147 U. S. 396. Harman *v.* Chicago 1892
163 U. S. 142. Illinois Central Ry. *v.* Illinois 1895
177 U. S. 514. Cleveland, Cincinnati, Chicago & St. Louis Ry. *v.* Illinois 1899
184 U. S. 540. Connolly *v.* Union Sewer Pipe Co. 1901
195 U. S. 1. Bradley *v.* Lightcap 1903
Total 11

Indiana—

14 Howard 268. Vincennes University *v.* Indiana 1852
122 U. S. 347. Western Union Tel. Co. *v.* Pendleton 1886
Total 2

Iowa—

e 11 Howard 437. Webster *v.* Reid 1850
h 4 Wall. 555. The Hine *v.* Trevor 1866

121 U. S. 186. Barron *v.* Burnside 1886
125 U. S. 465. Bowman *v.* Chicago & North W. Ry. Co...... 1887
135 U. S. 100. Leisy *v.* Hardin 1889
173 U. S. 193. Dewey *v.* Des Moines 1898
205 U. S. 503. Savings Bank *v.* Des Moines 1906
Total 7

Kansas—

5 Wall. 737. The Kansas Indians 1866
20 Wall. 655. Loan Association *v.* Topeka 1874
163 U. S. 118. Barnitz *v.* Beverly 1895
183 U. S. 79. Cotting *v.* Kansas City Stock Yards Co. 1901
216 U. S. 1. Western Union Tel. Co. *v.* Kansas 1909
217 U. S. 91. International Text Book Co. *v.* Pigg 1909
Total 6

Kentucky—

8 Wheaton 1. Greene *v.* Biddle 1823
115 U. S. 683. Louisville Gas Co. *v.* Citizens Gas Co. 1885
141 U. S. 47. Crutcher *v.* Kentucky 1890
154 U. S. 204. Covington & Cincinnati Bridge Co. *v.* Kentucky 1893
b 184 U. S. 27. Railroad Co. *v.* Eubank 1901
188 U. S. 385. Louisville Ferry Co. *v.* Kentucky 1902
199 U. S. 194. Union Transit Co. *v.* Kentucky 1905
206 U. S. 129. Express Co. *v.* Kentucky 1906
b 212 U. S. 132. Railroad Co. *v.* Stockyards Co. 1908
214 U. S. 218. Adams Express Co. *v.* Kentucky 1909
223 U. S. 70. Railroad Company *v.* Cook County 1911
Total 11

Louisiana—

4 Wheaton 209. McMillan *v.* McNeil 1819
6 Wall. 31. Steamship Co. *v.* Port Wardens 1867
b 14 Wall. 661. Delmas *v.* Insurance Co. 1871
a 20 Wall. 577. Cannon *v.* New Orleans 1874
94 U. S. 246. Foster *v.* Master of New Orleans 1876
95 U. S. 485. Hall *v.* DeCuir 1877
103 U. S. 358. Wolff *v.* New Orleans 1880
105 U. S. 278. Louisiana *v.* Pilsbury 1881
d 105 U. S. 362. Asylum *v.* New Orleans 1881
111 U. S. 716. Nelson *v.* St. Martin's Parish 1883
a 112 U. S. 69. Moran *v.* New Orleans 1884
d 115 U. S. 650. New Orleans Gas Co. *v.* Louisiana Light Co. 1885
g 115 U. S. 674. New Orleans Water Co. *v.* Rivers 1885
116 U. S. 131. Fisk *v.* Jefferson Police Jury 1885
165 U. S. 578. Allgeyer *v.* Louisiana 1896
215 U. S. 170. Hubert *v.* New Orleans 1909
Total 16

Maine—

2 Wall. 10. Hawthorne *v.* Calef 1864
Total 1

Maryland—

4 Wheaton 316. McCulloch *v.* Maryland 1819
12 Wheaton 419. Brown *v.* Maryland 1824
6 Peters 635. Boyle *v.* Zacharie.......................... 1832
3 Howard 133. Gordon *v.* The Tax Court 1845
12 Howard 293. Achison *v.* Huddleson 1851
12 Wall. 418. Ward *v.* Maryland 1870
c 100 U. S. 434. Guy *v.* Baltimore 1879
120 U. S. 502. Corson *v.* Maryland 1886
Total 8

Massachusetts—

[1] 7 Howard 283. Passenger Cases 1849
h 125 U. S. 530. Western Union Tel. Co. *v.* Massachusetts.... 1887
Total 2

Michigan—

116 U. S. 446. Walling *v.* Michigan 1885
121 U. S. 230. Fargo *v.* Michigan 1886
135 U. S. 161. Lyng *v.* Michigan 1889
173 U. S. 684. L. S. & M. S. Ry. Co. *v.* Smith 1898
a 184 U. S. 368. Detroit *v.* Detroit Citizens St. Ry. Co. 1902
201 U. S. 543. Powers *v.* Railroad Co. 1905
Total 6

Minnesota—

e 20 Howard 558. Irvine *v.* Marshall 1857
134 U. S. 418. Chicago, Milwaukee & St. Paul Ry. Co. *v.* Minnesota 1889
136 U. S. 313. Minnesota *v.* Barber 1889
179 U. S. 223. Stearns *v.* Minnesota 1900
179 U. S. 302. Duluth Iron Range Ry. *v.* St. Louis Co. 1900
209 U. S. 123. *Ex parte* Young 1907
a 215 U. S. 417. Minneapolis *v.* Minneapolis St. Ry. 1909
Total 7

Mississippi—

6 Howard 301. Planter's Bank *v.* Sharp 1848
5 Wall. 290. Christmas *v.* Russell 1866
c 202 U. S. 453. Vicksburg *v.* Waterworks Co. 1905
a 206 U. S. 496. Vicksburg *v.* Vicksburg Water Co. 1906
Total 4

[1] Listed also under New York.

Missouri—

4 Peters 410. Craig *v.* Missouri 1830
b 4 Wall. 277. Cummings *v.* Missouri 1866
8 Wall. 430. Home of the Friendless *v.* Rouse 1869
8 Wall. 439. Washington University *v.* Rouse 1869
13 Wall. 92. Gibson *v.* Choateau 1871
20 Wall. 36. Pacific Railway Co. *v.* McGuire 1873
91 U. S. 275. Welton *v.* State of Missouri 1875
95 U. S. 465. Railroad Co. *v.* Husen 1877
105 U. S. 733. Ralls County Court *v.* United States 1881
b 107 U. S. 221. Kring *v.* Missouri 1882
c 113 U. S. 1. Cole *v.* Lagrange 1884
122 U. S. 284. Seibert *v.* Lewis 1886
218 U. S. 135. Herndon *v.* Chicago, Rock Island Ry. 1909
Total 13

Montana—

e 11 Wall. 610. Dunphy *v.* Kleinsmith 1870
Total 1

Nebraska—

164 U. S. 403. Missouri Pacific Ry. Co. *v.* Nebraska 1896
169 U. S. 466. Smyth *v.* Ames 1897
217 U. S. 196. Missouri Pacific R. R. Co. *v.* Nebraska 1909
Total 3

Nevada—

6 Wall. 35. Crandall *v.* Nevada 1867
Total 1

New Hampshire—

4 Wheaton 518. Dartmouth College *v.* Woodward 1819
171 U. S. 30. Collins *v.* New Hampshire 1897
Total 2

New Jersey—

7 Cranch 164. New Jersey *v.* Wilson 1813
95 U. S. 104. New Jersey *v.* Yard 1877
Total 2

New Mexico—

New York—

4 Wheaton 122. Sturges *v.* Crowninshield 1819
9 Wheaton 1. Gibbons *v.* Ogden 1824
12 Wheaton 213. Ogden *v.* Saunders 1827
[1] 7 Howard 283. Passenger Cases 1849

[1] Listed also under Massachusetts.

2 Black 620.	Bank of Commerce *v.* New York City	1862
2 Wall. 200.	Bank Tax Case	1864
3 Wall. 51.	The Binghamton Bridge	1865
h 3 Wall. 573.	Van Allen *v.* The Assessors	1865
5 Wall. 761.	The New York Indians	1866
h 7 Wall. 26.	Bank *v.* The Supervisors	1868
92 U. S. 259.	Henderson *v.* New York	1875
94 U. S. 238.	Inman Steamship Co. *v.* Tinker	1876
107 U. S. 59.	People *v.* Compagnie Transatlantique	1882
191 U. S. 17.	The Robert W. Parsons	1903
198 U. S. 45.	Lochner *v.* New York	1904
212 U. S. 19.	Willcox *v.* Gas Co.	1908
	Total	16

North Carolina—

13 Wall. 264.	Wilmington Ry. *v.* Reid	1871
91 U. S. 3.	Wilmington & Weldon R. R. *v.* King	1875
d 96 U. S. 595.	Edwards *v.* Kearzey	1877
a 187 U. S. 622.	Caldwell *v.* North Carolina	1902
202 U. S. 543.	McNeil *v.* Southern Ry. Co.	1906
h 222 U. S. 424.	Southern Railroad Co. *v.* Reid	1911
	Total	6

North Dakota—

215 U. S. 515.	Flaherty *v.* Hansan	1909
	Total	1

Ohio—

h 9 Wheaton 738.	Osborn *v.* The U. S. Bank	1824
3 Howard 720.	Neil *v.* Ohio	1845
16 Howard 369.	State Bank *v.* Knoop	1853
18 Howard 331.	Dodge *v.* Woolsey	1855
127 U. S. 411.	Ratterman *v.* Western Union Tel. Co.	1887
a 172 U. S. 269.	Norwood *v.* Baker	1898
173 U. S. 276.	Ohio *v.* Thomas	1898
a 194 U. S. 517.	Cleveland *v.* Cleveland Ry. Co.	1903
a 201 U. S. 529.	Cleveland *v.* Cleveland R. R.	1905
	Total	9

Oklahoma—

221 U. S. 229.	Oklahoma *v.* Kansas Gas Co.	1910
223 U. S. 298.	Oklahoma *v.* Express Co.	1911
	Total	2

Oregon—

140 U. S. 1.	Pennoyer *v.* McConnaughy	1890
212 U. S. 315.	Nielson *v.* Oregon	1908
	Total	2

Pennsylvania—

5 Cranch 115.	United States *v.* Peters	1809
6 Wheaton 131.	Bank of Pa. *v.* Smith	1821
16 Peters 435.	Dobbins *v.* Com'rs of Erie County	1842
16 Peters 539.	Prigg *v.* Pennsylvania	1842
3 Howard 151.	Searight *v.* Stokes	1845
7 Wall. 262.	Railroad Co. *v.* Jackson	1868
15 Wall. 232.	State Freight Tax Case	1872
15 Wall. 300.	State Tax on Foreign-Held Bonds	1872
97 U. S. 566.	Cook *v.* Pennsylvania	1878
114 U. S. 196.	Gloucester Ferry Co. *v.* Pennsylvania	1884
122 U. S. 326.	Steamship Co. *v.* Pennsylvania	1886
136 U. S. 114.	Norfolk & Western Ry. Co. *v.* Pennsylvania.	1889
a 153 U. S. 289.	Brennan *v.* Titusville	1893
153 U. S. 628	Erie Railroad Co. *v.* Pennsylvania	1893
171 U. S. 1.	Schollenberger *v.* Pennsylvania	1897
a 192 U. S. 64.	Postal Telegraph *v.* Taylor	1903
a 203 U. S. 507.	Rearick *v.* Pennsylvania	1906
	Total	17

Rhode Island—

South Carolina—

a 2 Peters 449.	Weston *v.* City of Charleston	1829
19 Wall. 1.	Barings *v.* Dabney	1873
a 96 U. S. 432.	Murray *v.* Charleston	1877
165 U. S. 58.	Scott *v.* Donald	1896
	Total	4

South Dakota—

Tennessee—

8 Wall. 44.	Furman *v.* Nichol	1868
95 U. S. 679.	Farrington *v.* Tennessee	1877
97 U. S. 454.	Keith *v.* Clark	1878
117 U. S. 34.	Pickard *v.* Pullman Southern Car Co.	1885
117 U. S. 151.	Van Brocklin *v.* Tennessee	1885
120 U. S. 489.	Robbins *v.* Shelby Co. Taxing District	1886
153 U. S. 486.	Mobile & Ohio Ry. Co. *v.* Tennessee	1893
161 U. S. 134.	Bank of Commerce *v.* Tennessee	1895
172 U. S. 239.	Blake *v.* McClung	1898
185 U. S. 27.	Stockard *v.* Morgan	1901
191 U. S. 171.	Allen *v.* Pullman Co.	1903
208 U. S. 113.	Darnell *v.* Memphis	1907
	Total	12

Texas—

19 Wall. 581.	Peete *v.* Morgan	1873
102 U. S. 123.	Tiernan *v.* Rinker	1870
105 U. S. 460.	Telegraph Co. *v.* Texas	1881
128 U. S. 129.	Asher *v.* Texas	1888
h 158 U. S. 98.	Gulf Colorado & Santa Fe Ry. Co. *v.* Hefley	1894
165 U. S. 150.	Gulf Colorado & Santa Fe Ry. Co. *v.* Ellis	1896
b 170 U. S. 243.	Houston & Texas Central Ry. *v.* Texas	1897
177 U. S. 66.	Houston & Texas Central R. R. *v.* Texas	1898
201 U. S. 321.	Railroad Co. *v.* Mayes	1905
210 U. S. 217.	Railroad Co. *v.* Texas	1907
	Total	10

Utah—

e 166 U. S. 464.	American Publishing Co. *v.* Fisher	1896
b 170 U. S. 343.	Thompson *v.* Utah	1897
	Total	2

Vermont—

8 Wheaton 464.	Society, etc. *v.* New Haven	1823
	Total	1

Virginia—

9 Cranch 43.	Terrett *v.* Taylor	1815
102 U. S. 672.	Hartman *v.* Greennow	1880
103 U. S. 344.	Webber *v.* Virginia	1880
114 U. S. 270.	Virginia Coupon Cases	1884
115 U. S. 566.	Effinger *v.* Kenny	1885
116 U. S. 572.	Royall *v.* Virginia	1885
135 U. S. 662.	McGahey *v.* Virginia	1889
138 U. S. 78.	Brimmer *v.* Rebman	1890
141 U. S. 62.	Voight *v.* Wright	1890
	Total	9

Washington—

a 172 U. S. 1.	Walla Walla City *v.* Water Co.	1889
189 U. S. 185.	The Roanoke	1902
eh 222 U. S. 334.	Berryman *v.* Whitmore College	1911
h 222 U. S. 370.	Railroad Co. *v.* Washington	1911
	Total	4

West Virginia—

16 Wall. 234.	Pierce *v.* Carskadon	1872
100 U. S. 303.	Strauder *v.* West Virginia	1879
106 U. S. 487.	Parkersburg *v.* Brown	1882
	Total	3

Wisconsin—

20 Wall. 445. Insurance Co. *v.* Morse 1874
154 U. S. 626. Morrill *v.* Wisconsin 1876
103 U. S. 5. Hall *v.* Wisconsin 1880
Total 3

Wyoming—

District of Columbia—

129 U. S. 141. Stoutenburgh *v.* Hennick 1888
Total 1

a Municipal ordinance. b State constitution. c Statute and city ordinance. d Constitution and statute. e Territorial statute. g State constitution and municipal ordinance. h In conflict with United States statute which Congress had constitutional authority to enact.

APPENDIX V

Cases in which State Constitutions and Statutes, Territorial Statutes, and Municipal Ordinances were Nullified by the United States Supreme Court, Classified according to the Constitutional Clauses with which the Legislative Enactments Conflicted.[1]

"No state shall pass any law . . . impairing the obligation of contracts."

[2] 6 Cranch 87.	Fletcher *v.* Peck	Ga.	1810
7 Cranch 164.	New Jersey *v.* Wilson	N. J.	1812
4 Wheaton 122.	Sturges *v.* Crowninshield	N. Y.	1819
4 Wheaton 209.	McMillan *v.* McNeill	La.	1819
4 Wheaton 518.	Dartmouth College *v.* Woodward	N. H.	1819
6 Wheaton 131.	Bank *v.* Smith	Pa.	1821
8 Wheaton 1.	Green *v.* Biddle	Ky.	1823
1 Howard 311.	Bronson *v.* Kinzie	Ill.	1843
2 Howard 608.	McCracken *v.* Hayward	Ill.	1844
3 Howard 133.	Gordon *v.* The Tax Court	Md.	1845
6 Howard 301.	Planters Bank *v.* Sharp	Miss.	1848
10 Howard 190.	Woodruff *v.* Trapnall	Ark.	1850
14 Howard 268.	Vincennes University *v.* Indiana	Ind.	1852
15 Howard 304.	Curran *v.* Arkansas	Ark.	1853
16 Howard 369.	State Bank *v.* Knoop	Ohio	1853
18 Howard 331.	Dodge *v.* Woolsey	Ohio	1855
24 Howard 461.	Howard *v.* Bugbee	Ala.	1860
2 Wall. 10.	Hawthorne *v.* Calef	Me.	1862
3 Wall. 51.	The Binghamton Bridge	N. Y.	1865
4 Wall. 143.	McGee *v.* Mathis	Ark.	1866
4 Wall. 535.	Van Hoffman *v.* City of Quincy	Ill.	1866
8 Wall. 44.	Furman *v.* Nichol	Tenn.	1868

[1] In some instances a statute conflicted with more than one constitutional clause. In such instances the case is listed under the clause on which the court based the principal part of its argument.

[2] Also *ex post facto* and general principles.

8 Wall. 430.	Home of Friendless *v.* Rouse	Mo.	1869
8 Wall. 439.	Washington University *v.* Rouse	Mo.	1869
13 Wall. 264.	Wilmington Ry. *v.* Reid	N. C.	1871
13 Wall. 646.	White *v.* Hart	Ga.	1871
13 Wall. 654.	Osborn *v.* Nichol	Ark.	1871
14 Wall. 661.	Delmas *v.* Insurance Co.	La.	1871
15 Wall. 300.	State Tax on Foreign-Held Bonds	Pa.	1872
15 Wall. 610.	Gunn *v.* Barry	Ga.	1872
16 Wall. 244.	Humphrey *v.* Pegues	Ga.	1872
16 Wall. 314.	Walker *v.* Whitehead	Ga.	1872
19 Wall. 1.	Barings *v.* Dabney	S. C.	1873
20 Wall. 36.	Pacific Railway Co. *v.* McGuire	Mo.	1873
91 U. S. 3.	Wilmington & Weldon R. R. *v.* King	N. C.	1875
95 U. S. 104.	New Jersey *v.* Yard	N. J.	1877
95 U. S. 679.	Farrington *v.* Tennessee	Tenn.	1877
96 U. S. 432.	Murray *v.* Charleston	S. C.	1877
96 U. S. 595.	Edwards *v.* Kearzey	N. C.	1877
97 U. S. 454.	Keith *v.* Clark	Tenn.	1878
99 U. S. 309.	University *v.* People	Ill.	1878
102 U. S. 672.	Hartman *v.* Greennow	Va.	1880
103 U. S. 5.	Hall *v.* Wisconsin	Wis.	1880
103 U. S. 358.	Wolff *v.* New Orleans	La.	1880
105 U. S. 278.	Louisiana *v.* Pilsbury	La.	1881
105 U. S. 362.	Asylum *v.* New Orleans	La.	1881
105 U. S. 733.	Ralls County Court *v.* United States	Mo.	1881
111 U. S. 716.	Nelson *v.* St. Martin's Parish	La.	1883
114 U. S. 270.	Virginia Coupon Cases	Va.	1884
115 U. S. 566.	Effinger *v.* Kenny	Va.	1885
115 U. S. 650.	New Orleans Gas Co. *v.* Louisiana Light Compary	La.	1885
115 U. S. 674.	New Orleans Water Co. *v.* Rivers	La.	1885
115 U. S. 683.	Louisville Gas Co. *v.* Citizens Gas Co.	Ky.	1885
116 U. S. 131.	Fisk *v.* Jefferson Police Jury	La.	1885
116 U. S. 289.	Mobile *v.* Watson	Ala.	1885
116 U. S. 572.	Royall *v.* Virginia	Va.	1885
122 U. S. 284.	Seibert *v.* Lewis	Mo.	1886
135 U. S. 662.	McGahey *v.* Virginia	Va.	1889
140 U. S. 1.	Pennoyer *v.* McConnaughy	Ore.	1890
153 U. S. 486.	Mobile & Ohio Ry. Co. *v.* Tennessee	Tenn.	1893
153 U. S. 628.	Erie Railroad Co. *v.* Pennsylvania	Pa.	1893
161 U. S. 134.	Bank of Commerce *v.* Tennessee	Tenn.	1895
163 U. S. 118.	Barnitz *v.* Beverly	Kans.	1895
170 U. S. 243.	Houston & Texas Central Ry. *v.* Texas	Tex.	1897
172 U. S. 1.	Walla Walla *v.* Walla Walla Water Co.	Wash.	1898

177 U. S. 66. Railroad Co. *v.* Texas ....Tex. 1899
177 U. S. 558. Los Angeles *v.* Los Angeles Water Co..Cal. 1899
179 U. S. 223. Stearns *v.* Minnesota ....Minn. 1900
184 U. S. 368. Detroit *v.* Railway Co. ....Mich. 1901
194 U. S. 517. Cleveland *v.* Cleveland Ry. Co. ....Ohio 1903
195 U. S. 1. Bradley *v.* Lightcap ....Ill. 1903
201 U. S. 529. Cleveland *v.* Railway Co. ....Ohio 1905
201 U. S. 543. Powers *v.* Railroad Co. ....Mich. 1905
202 U. S. 453. Vicksburg *v.* Waterworks Co. ....Miss. 1905
204 U. S. 103. American Co. *v.* Colorado ....Col. 1906
206 U. S. 496. Vicksburg *v.* Vicksburg Water Co. ......Miss. 1906
215 U. S. 170. Hubert *v.* New Orleans ....La. 1909
215 U. S. 417. Minneapolis *v.* Minneapolis Ry. ....Minn. 1909
Total 78

Interstate and Foreign Commerce Clause.

9 Wheaton 1. Gibbons *v.* Ogden ....N. Y. 1824
[1] 12 Wheaton 419. Brown *v.* Maryland ....Md. 1827
7 Howard 283. Passenger Cases ....N. Y. & Mass. 1849
22 Howard 227. Sinnot *v.* Davenport ....Ala. 1859
6 Wall. 31. Steamship Co. *v.* Port Wardens ....La. 1867
15 Wall. 232. State Freight Tax Case ....Pa. 1872
91 U. S. 275. Welton *v.* Missouri ....Mo. 1875
92 U. S. 259. Henderson *v.* New York ....N. Y. 1875
92 U. S. 275. Chy Lung *v.* Freeman ....Cal. 1875
94 U. S. 246. Foster *v.* Master of New Orleans ....La. 1876
154 U. S. 626. Morrill *v.* Wisconsin ....Wis. 1876
95 U. S. 465. Railroad Co. *v.* Husen ....Mo. 1877
95 U. S. 485. Hall *v.* DeCuir ....La. 1877
96 U. S. 1. Pensacola Telegraph Co. *v.* Western Union Telegraph Co. ....Fla. 1877
97 U. S. 566. Cook *v.* Pennsylvania ....Pa. 1878
100 U. S. 434. Guy *v.* Baltimore ....Md. 1879
102 U. S. 123. Tiernan *v.* Rinker ....Tex. 1880
103 U. S. 344. Webber *v.* Virginia ....Va. 1880
105 U. S. 460. Telegraph Co. *v.* Texas ....Tex. 1881
107 U. S. 59. People *v.* Compagnie Transatlantique....N. Y. 1882
112 U. S. 69. Moran *v.* New Orleans ....La. 1884
114 U. S. 196. Gloucester Ferry Co. *v.* Pennsylvania ..Pa. 1884
116 U. S. 446. Walling *v.* Michigan ....Mich. 1885
117 U. S. 34. Pickard *v.* Pullman Car Co. ....Tenn. 1885
118 U. S. 90. Spraigue *v.* Thompson ....Ga. 1885
118 U. S. 557. Railroad Co. *v.* Illinois ....Ill. 1886

[1] Listed also under import and export clause.

120 U. S. 489.	Robbins *v.* Taxing District	Tenn.	1886
120 U. S. 502.	Corson *v.* Maryland	Md.	1886
121 U. S. 230.	Fargo *v.* Michigan	Mich.	1886
122 U. S. 326.	Steamship Co. *v.* Pennsylvania	Pa.	1886
122 U. S. 347.	Telegraph Co. *v.* Pendleton	Ind.	1886
125 U. S. 465.	Bowman *v.* Chicago & North. Ry. Co.	Iowa	1887
125 U. S. 530.	Western Union Tel. Co. *v.* Mass.	Mass.	1887
127 U. S. 411.	Ratterman *v.* Western Union Tel. Co.	Ohio	1887
127 U. S. 640.	Leloup *v.* Port of Mobile	Ala.	1887
128 U. S. 129.	Asher *v.* Texas	Tex.	1888
129 U. S. 141.	Stoutenburgh *v.* Hennick	D. C.	1888
132 U. S. 472.	Western Union Tel. Co. *v.* Alabama	Ala.	1889
135 U. S. 100.	Leisy *v.* Hardin	Iowa	1889
135 U. S. 161.	Lyng *v.* Michigan	Mich.	1889
136 U. S. 104.	McCall *v.* California	Cal.	1889
136 U. S. 114.	Railroad Co. *v.* Pennsylvania	Pa.	1889
136 U. S. 313.	Minnesota *v.* Barber	Minn.	1889
138 U. S. 78.	Brimmer *v.* Rebman	Va.	1890
141 U. S. 47.	Crutcher *v.* Kentucky	Ky.	1890
141 U. S. 62.	Voigt *v.* Wright	Va.	1890
147 U. S. 396.	Harman *v.* Chicago	Ill.	1892
153 U. S. 289.	Brennan *v.* Titusville	Pa.	1893
154 U. S. 204.	Covington & Cincinnati Bridge Co. *v.* Kentucky	Ky.	1893
158 U. S. 98.	Railroad Case *v.* Hefley	Tex.	1894
163 U. S. 142.	Illinois Central Ry. *v.* Illinois	Ill.	1895
165 U. S. 58.	Scott *v.* Donald	S. C.	1896
171 U. S. 1.	Schollenberger *v.* Pennsylvania	Pa.	1897
171 U. S. 30.	Collins *v.* New Hampshire	N. H.	1897
177 U. S. 514.	Railroad Co. *v.* Illinois	Ill.	1899
184 U. S. 27.	Railroad Co. *v.* Eubank	Ky.	1901
185 U. S. 27.	Stockard *v.* Morgan	Tenn.	1901
187 U. S. 622.	Caldwell *v.* North Carolina	N. C.	1902
191 U. S. 171.	Allen *v.* Pullman Co.	Tenn.	1903
192 U. S. 64.	Postal Telegraph Co. *v.* Taylor	Pa.	1904
196 U. S. 194.	Central Ry. of Georgia *v.* Murphey	Ga.	1904
201 U. S. 321.	Railroad Co. *v.* Mayes	Tex.	1905
202 U. S. 543.	McNeil *v.* Southern R. R. Co.	N. C.	1906
203 U. S. 507.	Rearick *v.* Pennsylvania	Pa.	1906
206 U. S. 129.	Express Co. *v.* Kentucky	Ky.	1906
208 U. S. 113.	Darnell *v.* Memphis	Tenn.	1907
210 U. S. 217.	Railroad Co. *v.* Texas	Tex.	1907
214 U. S. 218.	Adams Express Co. *v.* Kentucky	Ky.	1909
216 U. S. 1.	Telegraph Co. *v.* Kansas	Kans.	1909

216 U. S. 146.	Ludwig *v.* Telegraph Co.	Ark.	1909
217 U. S. 91.	Text Book Co. *v.* Pigg	Kans.	1909
217 U. S. 136.	Railroad Co. *v.* Arkansas	Ark.	1909
218 U. S. 124.	Dozier *v.* Alabama	Ala.	1909
221 U. S. 229.	Oklahoma *v.* Kansas Gas Co.	Okla.	1910
222 U. S. 370.	Railroad Co. *v.* Washington	Wash.	1911
222 U. S. 424.	Railroad Co. *v.* Reid	N. C.	1911
223 U. S. 70.	Railroad Co. *v.* Cook County	Ky.	1911
223 U. S. 280.	Railroad Co. *v.* O'Connor	Col.	1911
223 U. S. 298.	Oklahoma *v.* Express Co.	Okla.	1911
	Total		79

General—No specific clause indicated, or miscellaneous.

5 Cranch 115.	United States *v.* Peters	Pa.	1809
9 Cranch 43.	Terrett *v.* Taylor	Va.	1815
4 Wheaton 316.	McCulloch *v.* Maryland	Md.	1819
8 Wheaton 464.	Society, etc. *v.* New Haven	Vt.	1823
9 Wheaton 738.	Osborn *v.* The United States Bank	Ohio	1824
12 Wheaton 213.	Ogden *v.* Saunders	N. Y.	1827
2 Peters 449.	Weston *v.* Charleston	S. C.	1829
6 Peters 635.	Boyle *v.* Zacharie	Md.	1832
16 Peters 435.	Dobbins *v.* Commissioners	Pa.	1842
3 Howard 151.	Searight *v.* Stokes	Pa.	1845
3 Howard 720.	Neil *v.* Ohio	Ohio	1845
12 Howard 293.	Achison *v.* Huddleson	Md.	1851
17 Howard 596.	Hays *v.* Pacific Mail Co.	Cal.	1854
20 Howard 558.	Irvine *v.* Marshall	Minn.	1857
2 Black 620.	Bank of Commerce *v.* New York City	N. Y.	1862
2 Wall. 200.	Bank Tax Case	N. Y.	1864
3 Wall. 573.	Van Allen *v.* Assessors	N. Y.	1865
4 Wall. 411.	The Moses Taylor	Cal.	1866
4 Wall. 459.	Bradley *v.* The People	Ill.	1866
4 Wall. 555.	The Hine *v.* Trevor	Iowa	1866
6 Wall. 35.	Crandall *v.* Nevada	Nev.	1867
7 Wall. 26.	Bank *v.* Supervisors	N. Y.	1868
7 Wall. 262.	Railroad Co. *v.* Jackson	Pa.	1868
7 Wall. 624.	The Belfast	Ala.	1868
11 Wall. 610.	Dunphy *v.* Kleinsmith	Mont.	1870
13 Wall. 92.	Gibson *v.* Chouteau	Mo.	1871
20 Wall. 445.	Insurance Co. *v.* Morse	Wis.	1874
20 Wall. 655.	Loan Association *v.* Topeka	Kans.	1874
106 U. S. 487.	Parkersburg *v.* Brown	W. Va.	1882
113 U. S. 1.	Cole *v.* LaGrange	Mo.	1884
117 U. S. 151.	Van Brocklin *v.* Tenn.	Tenn.	1885
121 U. S. 186.	Barron *v.* Burnsides	Iowa	1886

127 U. S. 1.	California *v.* Central Pacific R. R. Co.	Cal.	1887
173 U. S. 276.	Ohio *v.* Thomas	Ohio	1898
189 U. S. 185.	The Roanoke	Wash.	1902
191 U. S. 17.	The Robert W. Parsons	N. Y.	1903
205 U. S. 503.	Savings Bank *v.* Des Moines	Iowa	1906
212 U. S. 315.	Nielson *v.* Oregon	Ore.	1908
215 U. S. 515.	Flaherty *v.* Hanson	N. D.	1909
218 U. S. 135.	Herndon *v.* Railroad Co.	Mo.	1909
222 U. S 334.	Berryman *v.* Whitman College	Wash.	1911
		Total	41

No state shall "deprive any person of life, liberty, or property, without due process of law."

[1] 134 U. S. 418.	Railroad Co. *v.* Minnesota	Minn.	1889
164 U. S. 403.	Railroad Co. *v.* Nebraska	Nebr.	1896
[2] 165 U. S. 150.	Railroad Co. *v.* Ellis	Tex.	1896
165 U. S. 578.	Allgeyer *v.* Louisiana	La.	1896
[2] 169 U. S. 466.	Smyth *v.* Ames	Nebr.	1897
[2] 172 U. S. 269.	Norwood *v.* Baker	Ohio	1898
[2] 173 U. S. 193.	Dewey *v.* Des Moines	Iowa	1898
173 U. S. 684.	Railroad Co. *v.* Smith	Mich.	1898
179 U. S. 302.	Railroad Co. *v.* St. Louis Co.	Minn.	1900
188 U. S. 385.	Ferry Co. *v.* Kentucky	Ky.	1902
[2] 195 U. S. 223.	Dobbins *v.* Los Angeles	Cal.	1904
[2] 198 U. S. 45.	Lochner *v.* New York	N. Y.	1904
199 U. S. 194.	Union Transfer Co. *v.* Kentucky	Ky.	1904
207 U. S. 127.	Railroad Co. *v.* Wright	Ga.	1907
[2] 209 U. S. 123.	*Ex parte* Young	Minn.	1907
210 U. S. 217.	Railroad Co. *v.* Texas	Tex.	1907
[2] 212 U. S. 19.	Willcox *v.* Gas Co.	N. Y.	1908
212 U. S. 132.	Railroad Co. *v.* Stockyards	Ky.	1908
217 U. S. 196.	Railroad Co. *v.* Nebraska	Nebr.	1910
		Total	19

Equal protection clause.

100 U. S. 303.	Strauder *v.* West Virginia	W. Va.	1879
118 U. S. 356.	Yick Wo *v.* Hopkins	Cal.	1885
183 U. S. 79.	Cotting *v.* Stock Yards	Kan.	1901
184 U. S. 540.	Connolly *v.* Sewer Pipe Co.	Ill.	1901
216 U. S. 400.	Railroad Co. *v.* Greene	Ala.	1909
		Total	5

[1] Equal protection also mentioned but case based mainly on due process.

[2] Decision based on 14th Amendment.

Thirteenth Amendment.

219 U. S. 219.	Bailey *v.* Alabama	Ala.	1910
		Total	1

Bills of Attainder.

[1] 4 Wall. 277.	Cummings *v.* Missouri	Mo.	1865
16 Wall. 234.	Pierce *v.* Carskadon	W. Va.	1872
		Total	2

"*Full faith and credit shall be given in each state to the public acts, records, and judicial proceedings of every other state.*"

5 Wall. 290.	Christmas *v.* Russell	Miss.	1866
		Total	1

"*In suits at common law, where the value in controversy shall exceed twenty dollars, the right of trial by jury shall be preserved.*"

[2] 11 Howard 437.	Webster *v.* Reid	Iowa	1850
[2] 166 U. S. 464.	Publishing Co. *v.* Fisher	Utah	1896
		Total	2

"*No state . . . shall pass any . . . ex post facto law.*"

[3] 4 Wall. 277.	Cummings *v.* Missouri	Mo.	1866
107 U. S. 221.	Kring *v.* Missouri	Mo.	1882
134 U. S. 160.	*Ex parte* Medley	Col.	1889
170 U. S. 343.	Thompson *v.* Utah	Utah	1897
		Total	4

Infringement on the treaty-making power of the United States.

6 Peters 515.	Worcester *v.* Georgia	Ga.	1832
5 Wall. 737.	The Kansas Indians	Kan.	1866
5 Wall. 761.	The New York Indians	N. Y.	1866
		Total	3

"*No person held to service or labor in one state, under the laws thereof, escaping into another, shall, in consequence of any law or regulation therein, be discharged from such service or labor; but shall be delivered up, on claim of the party to whom such service or labor may be due.*"

16 Peters 539.	Prigg *v.* Pennsylvania	Pa.	1842
		Total	1

[1] Also listed under *ex post facto* clause.

[2] Territorial statutes.

[3] Also listed under bill of attainder clause.

"No state shall, without the consent of Congress, lay any duty of tonnage."

12 Wall. 204.	State Tonnage Tax Cases	Ala.	1870
19 Wall. 581.	Peete *v.* Morgan	Tex.	1873
20 Wall. 577.	Cannon *v.* New Orleans	La.	1874
94 U. S. 238.	Inman Steamship Co. *v.* Tinker	N. Y.	1876
	Total		4

"The citizens of each state shall be entitled to all privileges and immunities of citizens in the several states."

12 Wall. 418.	Ward *v.* Maryland	Md.	1870
172 U. S. 239.	Blake *v.* McClung	Tenn.	1898
	Total		2

"No state shall, without the consent of Congress, lay any imposts or duties on imports or exports," etc.

[1] 12 Wheaton 419.	Brown *v.* Maryland	Md.	1827
24 Howard 169.	Almy *v.* California	Cal.	1860
	Total		2

"No state shall . . . emit bills of credit."

4 Peters 410.	Craig *v.* Missouri	Mo.	1830
	Total		1

STATISTICAL SUMMARY

	Contract Clause	Interstate and Foreign Commerce	General	14th Amendment	All others	Total
1790–1800 ..	..	..	..		..	.
1800–1810 ..	1	..	1		..	2
1810–1820 ..	4	..	2		..	6
1820–1830 ..	2	2	4		2	10
1830–1840 ..	..	..	1		1	2
1840–1850 ..	5	1	3		2	11
1850–1860 ..	5	1	3		1	10
1860–1870 ..	7	1	11		7	26
1870–1880 ..	20	13	3	1	4	41
1880–1890 ..	15	28	5	2	2	52
1890–1900 ..	9	9	1	8	3	30
1900–1910 ..	10	19	6	13	1	49
1910–1911 ..	..	5	1	..	..	6
	78	79	41	24	23	245

[1] Also listed under interstate commerce clause.

Printed in the USA
CPSIA information can be obtained
at www.ICGtesting.com
LVHW091736010224
770556LV00002B/123

9 781616 191474